# DETROIT
# RED WINGS
# TRIVIA TEASERS

RICHARD PENNINGTON

TRAILS BOOKS
Madison, Wisconsin

©2007 Richard Pennington

Library of Congress Control Number: 2007932371
ISBN: 978-1-931599-93-1

Editor: Mark Knickelbine
Designer: Colin Harrington
Photo Credits: cover right, pages iv, 14, and 40, Hockey Hall of Fame; pages 54 and 86, Imperial Oil-Turofsky/Hockey Hall of Fame; cover left, page 122, Portnoy/Hockey Hall of Fame.

Printed in the United States of America.
12 11 10 09 08 07          6 5 4 3 2 1

Trails Books, a division of Big Earth Publishing
923 Williamson Street • Madison, WI 53703
(800) 258-5830 • www.trailsbooks.com

# TABLE OF
# CONTENTS

Fans line up to see the Wings play in "the Old Red Barn".

# CHAPTER ONE
# THE COUGARS AND THE FALCONS

There had been pro baseball (a team called the Wolverines, followed, of course, by the Tigers) in Detroit, beginning in 1881. And pro football (the Heralds, then the Lions) came upon the scene in 1920; the Pistons did not move from Fort Wayne, Indiana, to Detroit until 1957. Despite an abundance of winter ice—and sporting young men—hockey for any kind of payment did not occur in southeastern Michigan until relatively late. Nevertheless, the state can boast a member of the first loose grouping of pro teams—the International Hockey League, which began play in 1905. Sault Ste. Marie, in the Upper Peninsula, had a team known as the Soos.

A step up from that was the National Hockey League, formed in 1917. Not until seven years later did this quartet of Canadian teams grant an American franchise. The Boston Bruins were followed soon by the Pittsburgh Pirates and New York Americans. The really momentous year was 1926, when a couple of Midwestern cities—Chicago and Detroit—got teams, and New York got its second (the Rangers).

One of the NHL's competitors, the Western Canadian Hockey League, was going out of business. It sold many of its assets to the NHL, especially the contracts of all its players, for $258,000. The roster of the Portland Rosebuds was shifted to Chicago and became the Black Hawks, whereas the Victoria Cougars kept their nickname but moved to Detroit. And why not? Detroit was a booming city of more than 900,000, home of the auto industry, aspiring to greatness of all kinds. The enduring and galvanizing presence of Ty Cobb and the Detroit Tigers could not have been lost on anyone; perhaps that would happen in hockey, too.

It should be noted that no fewer than five groups from Detroit had made pitches for a franchise at the NHL's 1926 spring meeting. The one that prevailed was led by Charles Hughes. He spoke for a syndicate of 73 local investors, which included such heavyweights as Edsel Ford, S.S. Kresge, and William E. Scripps. A man with considerable powers of persuasion, Hughes convinced the Detroit

Athletic Club and other civic boosters to bring pro hockey to town. Over the previous winter, he had put on some exhibitions featuring NHL clubs, and they had drawn reasonably well.

The Detroit Cougars came into existence on October 5, 1926, but they had no suitable rink. Their first year of competition would be held not in Detroit, not in Michigan, not even in the United States. Home games were played across the Detroit River in Windsor, Ontario. They played at the Border Cities Arena, which still stands today. Built of wood in 1924 for the local junior hockey team, it had a seating capacity of 6,000, which was expanded to 9,000 for the Cougars. The rink, since renamed Windsor Arena, is an asymmetrical 80' x 195'.

How good was that first team in franchise history?

Although the Victoria Cougars had won the 1925 Stanley Cup and were Cup finalists the next year, they didn't do too well after the transfer—12 wins, 28 losses, and 4 ties. It was the worst record in the NHL in the 1927 season.

Did they make a profit?

On the contrary, the Detroit Cougars were $84,000 in debt after just one year.

Who was Detroit's first coach?

 Art Duncan. With Vancouver, he had led the Pacific Coast Hockey Association in scoring in 1924. Duncan, who served as player-manager in Detroit, was there for the first 33 games of the 1927 season. He went straight to Toronto and coached there, winning the Stanley Cup in 1932.

 Name four players who made the move from Victoria to Detroit.

 Harry "Hap" Holmes, Frank Frederickson, Jack Walker, and Frank Foyston.

 What distinction does Holmes hold?

 He was the first goalie to win the Stanley Cup with four different franchises—the Toronto Blueshirts, Toronto Arenas (later the St. Pats and finally the Maple Leafs), Seattle Metropolitans, and Victoria Cougars.

And Walker?

  He was a teammate of Holmes, sharing in three of those championships—with the Blueshirts, Metropolitans, and Cougars. Walker's playing career began in 1906 and did not end until 1932.

  Who did *not* make the trip from Victoria to Detroit?

Lester Patrick, "the Silver Fox." He was a player-coach with the Cougars in 1925 and 1926, but he had what he considered a better offer than that of Detroit. He would play for, then coach and serve as GM of the New York Rangers until 1946, guiding them to three Stanley Cups.

What was the first player transaction in Detroit Red Wings history?

In 1927, the team sent Frank Frederickson and Harry Meeking to Boston, in exchange for Gordon "Duke" Keats and Archie Briden.

He started playing pro hockey at age 17 for $75 a month, fought in World War I, and came back home to resume a long and distinguished career, albeit one that included just three NHL seasons. Who was this man with a reputation as a magnificent puck handler?

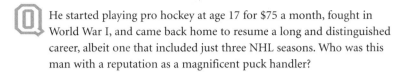 Duke Keats, a Montreal native. He had one season each with Boston, Detroit, and Chicago. Keats, once praised by NHL pioneer Lester Patrick as "the brainiest pivot that ever strapped on a skate" served as the team's interim coach for the final 11 games of the 1927 season.

 Who was the first player in team history to score a hat trick?

 Keats scored three goals against Pittsburgh on March 10, 1927.

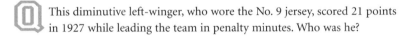

 This diminutive left-winger, who wore the No. 9 jersey, scored 21 points in 1927 while leading the team in penalty minutes. Who was he?

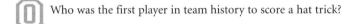 Johnny Sheppard. It was he who scored the first goal in the history of Olympia Stadium, putting a shot past Ottawa Senators goalie Alex Connell on November 22, 1927. Sheppard, whose younger brother Frank was also on that team, was a rugged competitor who once worked as a trapper near the Arctic Circle. Despite his contributions, he was soon traded to the New York Americans in exchange for $12,500, Bobby Connors, and the rights to promising amateur Ebbie Goodfellow.

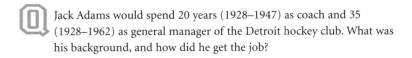 Jack Adams would spend 20 years (1928–1947) as coach and 35 (1928–1962) as general manager of the Detroit hockey club. What was his background, and how did he get the job?

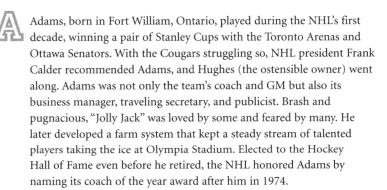 Adams, born in Fort William, Ontario, played during the NHL's first decade, winning a pair of Stanley Cups with the Toronto Arenas and Ottawa Senators. With the Cougars struggling so, NHL president Frank Calder recommended Adams, and Hughes (the ostensible owner) went along. Adams was not only the team's coach and GM but also its business manager, traveling secretary, and publicist. Brash and pugnacious, "Jolly Jack" was loved by some and feared by many. He later developed a farm system that kept a steady stream of talented players taking the ice at Olympia Stadium. Elected to the Hockey Hall of Fame even before he retired, the NHL honored Adams by naming its coach of the year award after him in 1974.

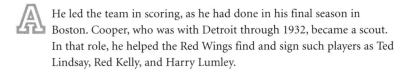 After he came over from the Bruins in a 1927 trade, how did Carson Cooper do in his first three years with the Cougars?

 He led the team in scoring, as he had done in his final season in Boston. Cooper, who was with Detroit through 1932, became a scout. In that role, he helped the Red Wings find and sign such players as Ted Lindsay, Red Kelly, and Harry Lumley.

Jack Adams ignored rumors that this man was washed up, obtaining him from the Montreal Maroons for $7,500 in 1927. Who was he?

 Reg Noble, who was immediately named captain of the team. A gritty competitor who switched from left wing to defense, Noble was well known to Adams since they had been teammates in Toronto a decade earlier. At one time, he led the NHL in career assists. Noble's final NHL season was 1933, which made him one of the few players to perform for Detroit as a Cougar, a Falcon, and a Red Wing. The last active player from the NHL's inaugural season of 1918, he later served as a referee.

 What was Jack Adams' line about buying Howie Morenz from the Montreal Canadiens?

 Morenz was probably hockey's first bonafide superstar. Adams said that if Detroit were able to buy him for $1.98, it still could not afford to do so. The hockey club was in dire financial straits in the late 1920s and early 1930s before James Norris, Sr., bought it in 1932. The players lost more than they won; they were poorly paid; they traveled by day coach; and their post-game spread usually consisted of cheese sandwiches.

 Million-dollar Olympia Stadium, "the Old Red Barn," was designed by architect C. Howard Crane and built at 5920 Grand River Avenue in time for the 1928 season. With a seating capacity of 11,563 (expanded to 13,375 in 1966 and capable of holding another 3,000 standing-room patrons), it was a landmark and home to the franchise for the next half-century. How did this edifice come to be built?

 A power struggle took place between two groups of sports-minded businessmen. One wanted an arena constructed across from the old Ford Motor Company plant in Highland Park, but another—which included Henry Ford and his friends at the Detroit Athletic Club— disagreed and set about building their own. Within a year, the Olympia had been designed, constructed, and opened.

What else happened at the Olympia besides pro hockey?

 It opened with a rodeo in September 1927, was a major venue for wrestling and boxing (Joe Louis, Jake LaMotta, Sugar Ray Robinson, Jersey Joe Walcott, Ezzard Charles, Thomas Hearns, and many others fought there). The Detroit Pistons played there from 1957 to 1961, and countless musical acts (such as Frank Sinatra, Elvis Presley, the Beatles, the Rolling Stones, Pink Floyd, and Traffic) appeared there as well.

 Was the Olympia a good place to watch a hockey game?

 It certainly was. Built of steel, poured concrete, and red brick, Olympia Stadium featured several tiers, had excellent sight lines, and was fan-friendly before that cliché had been invented. Tremendous noise could be generated there when the Red Wings were going good.

 Who took over Detroit's goaltending duties from 1929 to 1931?

 Clarence "Dolly" Dolson, who won a total of 35 games during those years.

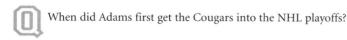 When did Adams first get the Cougars into the NHL playoffs?

That came in 1929, although they remained among the league's have-nots and were constantly on the verge of bankruptcy. Tight-fisted and indecisive ownership characterized the franchise's early years as Detroit made the playoffs just twice in its first seven seasons, losing in the first round both times.

Who scored the first goal in Detroit playoff history in a 1929 Stanley Cup game against Toronto?

Left-winger George Hay, then the finest stickhandler in hockey. He had come over from Chicago after the 1927 season. Hay recovered from an arm injury and scored 35 points to lead the 1928 team. Although he was named captain in 1931, Hay was nearing the end. After the 1934 season, he became a coach for Detroit's farm club in London, Ontario. Sandwiching Hay's hockey career was service in both world wars.

Upon Hay's retirement as a player, what did *Detroit News* sportswriter Sam Green have to say about him?

"He ranked with the great forwards of the game, combining speed and poise, aggressiveness and finesse, with unsurpassed mechanical ability." Adams, too, had high praise for Hay.

The 1929 team was not exactly an offensive juggernaut. How many goals did they score?

 Jack Adams' second team scored just 72 goals in 44 games; this was before forward passing was allowed, which had the effect of keeping scores very low. Carson Cooper scored 18 of those goals, fourth best in the league.

 After being obtained from the New York Americans, he led Detroit in scoring in 1931 and 1932, yet Adams asked him to switch to defense. For the good of the team, he agreed. Who was this good fellow?

 Ebenezer "Ebbie" Goodfellow. With him patrolling the blueline, Detroit won back-to-back Stanley Cups in 1936 and 1937. Three times an All-Star at his adopted position, Goodfellow also won the Hart Trophy as the NHL's most valuable player in 1940—the first Red Wings player to be so honored.

 Name the other players in this franchise to have won the Hart Trophy.

Sid Abel (1949), Gordie Howe (1952, 1953, 1957, 1958, 1960, 1963), and Sergei Fedorov (1994).

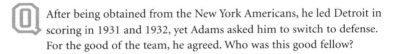

In an attempt to alter the team's identity, management wanted a new name. What would it be?

 They were called the Detroit Falcons for two seasons—1931 and 1932. The nickname was the result of a contest held by the city's three local newspapers. Of the 2,000 entries, 92 picked "Falcons." The team colors were gold and white.

 He had played baseball, football, and lacrosse during his younger days and did not learn hockey until he was serving in World War I. He was a quick study, though, and proved quite adept as a goaltender, helping the Ottawa Senators win the 1927 Stanley Cup. Who was he, and when was he in Detroit?

 Alex Connell is the man in question, and he was with the Falcons just one year—1932. After a brief retirement, he joined the Montreal Maroons and won another championship. One of the first goalies to record a 30-win season, he still holds the NHL record for longest shutout streak at 461 minutes, 29 seconds (more than six games). Connell's 1.99 career goals-against average is the best among goaltenders of his era.

 The NHL's Ottawa team folded after the 1932 season. Which of the Senators' players came to Detroit as a result?

Alex Connell, Hec Kilrea, Alex Smith, Danny Cox, and Art Gagne. As if that were not enough, the players from the Chicago Shamrocks of the American Hockey League also came to Detroit.

Why did the league permit this?

 The Falcons were bankrupt and had gone into receivership. The merged teams were good enough to reach the NHL quarterfinals again, falling in two games to the Montreal Maroons.

 What happened in team history on April 28, 1932?

 The Union Guardian Trust Company filed a notice of default against Detroit Hockey Club Incorporated, ordering it to pay $776,770. When that debt was not paid, the mortgage on Olympia Stadium was foreclosed and the company took possession of the team and its home.

1936 Stanley Cup winners

# CHAPTER TWO
# THE WINGED WHEEL
# BEGINS TO ROLL

The savior of Detroit's wobbly NHL franchise was born in 1879 in St. Catherines, Ontario, but grew up in a suburb of Montreal. James Norris' family was quite wealthy, possessing a number of grain, shipping, cattle, and real estate companies. He was 18 when his father moved the family and business from Montreal to Chicago. The younger Norris proved equally adept in the business world, becoming the top cash grain buyer in the world in the 1930s with a net worth in excess of $250 million.

He had been a good athlete in his younger days, specializing in hockey, squash, and tennis. A defenseman at McGill University (where the first known set of ice hockey rules was drawn up in the 1870s) and with the Montreal Amateur Athletic Association (four-time winner of the Stanley Cup before the Cup became the exclusive domain of the National Hockey League), Norris wanted to own a team—but not the one in Detroit. He had sought originally to buy the expansion Chicago Black Hawks. Now a resident of the Windy City, he often criticized owner Frederic McLaughlin and was planning to organize a team there in an upstart league. But NHL president Frank Calder brought that matter to a halt by convincing the other owners to let Norris buy the woeful Detroit Falcons, who were then in receivership. Paying $5 million for the franchise and Olympia Stadium, Norris cleared away the debt, and the team was on its way to becoming a powerhouse in pro hockey. Under his watch, they would win five Stanley Cups.

Norris wasted no time in renaming them the Red Wings. He also designed the team's logo—a red-and-white wing protruding from a wheel. The logo was adapted from that of the MAAA (the team was known as the "Winged Wheelers") and was meant to curry favor with the city's automobile companies. Henry Ford was said to be pleased.

According to the *Canadian Press*, "Big Jim always liked a hard-hitting team and invariably during his ownership, the Red Wings were just that. Players like Ebbie Goodfellow and 'Black Jack' Stewart were the apple of his eye." After his death in December 1952, the NHL honored this giant of the game with the annual presentation of the Norris Trophy to the top defenseman, and in 1974 one of its four divisions was named after him. His children, James, Jr., Bruce, and Marguerite, were involved—not always amicably so—in the operation of the Red Wings. All told, the Norris family owned the team for a half-century, from 1932 to 1982.

 Did Norris attend all of the Wings' games?

 On the contrary, he seldom did, due to a heart condition. So after every game, coach and general manager Jack Adams would call Norris from the locker room and give him the results.

 What goalie was known as "Little Napoleon"?

 John Ross Roach. Just 5' 5" and weighing 130 pounds, Roach had seven good years with the Toronto St. Pats/Maple Leafs and four with the New York Rangers before coming to the Motor City in 1932 for $11,000. A feisty and acrobatic player for all those seasons, Roach was showing signs of age and wear by 1934 and soon hung up his skates.

 Carl Voss (1933) was Detroit's first winner of the Calder Trophy, signifying the rookie of the year. Who were the others?

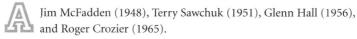 Jim McFadden (1948), Terry Sawchuk (1951), Glenn Hall (1956), and Roger Crozier (1965).

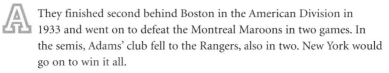 When did the Red Wings finally win a Stanley Cup playoff game?

They finished second behind Boston in the American Division in 1933 and went on to defeat the Montreal Maroons in two games. In the semis, Adams' club fell to the Rangers, also in two. New York would go on to win it all.

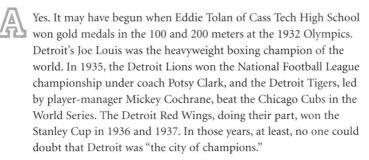 Detroit was hard hit during the Great Depression, with more than 220,000 people out of work. Some homeowners were unable to pay their mortgages or property taxes, banks were closing right and left, and a fiscal crisis gripped the city. Was there good news on the sporting scene?

Yes. It may have begun when Eddie Tolan of Cass Tech High School won gold medals in the 100 and 200 meters at the 1932 Olympics. Detroit's Joe Louis was the heavyweight boxing champion of the world. In 1935, the Detroit Lions won the National Football League championship under coach Potsy Clark, and the Detroit Tigers, led by player-manager Mickey Cochrane, beat the Chicago Cubs in the World Series. The Detroit Red Wings, doing their part, won the Stanley Cup in 1936 and 1937. In those years, at least, no one could doubt that Detroit was "the city of champions."

Red Wings goalie John Ross Roach had suffered a facial injury early in the 1934 season, so Adams worked a "loan" arrangement with the Montreal Canadiens. Who did he get for help between the pipes?

 He got Wilf Cude. Welsh-born and Winnipeg-raised, Cude did not have a very distinguished hockey résumé but he came through for the Wings in '34. An acrobatic netminder and a fiery competitor, he went 10-2-8 in his first 20 games as a Red Wing, with three shutouts. He finished that season with an NHL-leading 1.52 goals-against average, as the Wings won the American Division. Cude's 1-0 shutout victory over Toronto in the fifth and deciding game of the semifinals moved the Wings into their first Stanley Cup final, against the Black Hawks. Chicago took the series in four games. Cude, who had proved his value under pressure, was recalled by the Canadiens and was their main goaltender for the next five years.

 A magician with the puck, this man played for Detroit in 1934 and 1935. But he was best known for helping the Boston Bruins win their first Stanley Cup in 1929 as a rookie. The next year, he won the points title with 73, easily breaking Howie Morenz's single-season scoring record of 51. He later returned to Boston, coaching the Bruins when they swept Detroit in the 1941 Stanley Cup finals. Who was he?

 Ralph "Cooney" Weiland. He also coached hockey at Harvard from 1950 to 1971.

 Following the institution of the NHL's penalty shot rule, only one of the Red Wings' first 15 shots was good. Who did it?

 On December 13, 1934, Ebbie Goodfellow connected against St. Louis goaltender Bill Beveridge.

He had been the top scorer for a team in Duluth, so Jack Adams took him in the 1928 inter-league draft. He blossomed in a career that spanned 11 years, all of them in Detroit. Who was this fast and gentlemanly player?

Herbie Lewis. Seven times he collected at least 30 points, peaking in 1935 with 43. He was alleged to have the NHL's top salary at the time—$8,000. When Adams got Marty Barry from Boston to augment Lewis and Larry Aurie, the trio worked well together, sparking Detroit to two Cup wins.

The financially stressed Ottawa Senators had moved to St. Louis in 1935 and played as the St. Louis Eagles for one year before folding. What good fortune resulted from this event for the Red Wings?

For $50,000, the Eagles sold Syd Howe and Ralph "Scotty" Bowman (not to be confused with the man of the same name who would coach the Wings to Stanley Cups in 1997, 1998, and 2002) to Detroit. Both would contribute mightily to the success of the franchise in the years to come.

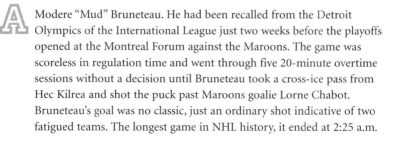

A rookie right-winger needed just one game in the 1936 Stanley Cup playoffs to cement his place in the lore of the Battered Mug. Name this native of St. Boniface, Manitoba.

Modere "Mud" Bruneteau. He had been recalled from the Detroit Olympics of the International League just two weeks before the playoffs opened at the Montreal Forum against the Maroons. The game was scoreless in regulation time and went through five 20-minute overtime sessions without a decision until Bruneteau took a cross-ice pass from Hec Kilrea and shot the puck past Maroons goalie Lorne Chabot. Bruneteau's goal was no classic, just an ordinary shot indicative of two fatigued teams. The longest game in NHL history, it ended at 2:25 a.m.

Who was Detroit's goalie for that 176-minute affair in '36?

 Norman "Normie" Smith, who stopped 89 shots on goal that night. Winner of the Vezina Trophy (top goaltender) in 1937, Smith suffered an arm injury and slumped in 1938 as the Red Wings finished last. Adams traded him to Boston soon thereafter. Smith retired and came back to Detroit when World War II sapped the NHL of so many players.

 What other Detroit goalies have won the Vezina Trophy?

 John Mowers (1943) and Terry Sawchuk (1952, 1953, and 1955).

 How long did Bruneteau stay with the Wings?

 He spent 11 productive seasons in Detroit, three times scoring more than 20 goals, including a career-high 35 in 1944. A clever winger and a solid two-way hockey player, he appeared in 411 games, scored 139 goals, and handed out 138 assists. His brother Ed was a Wing too for most of the 1940s.

Name the roster of the 1936 Stanley Cup champion Detroit Red Wings.

 John Sorrell, Syd Howe, Marty Barry, Herbie Lewis, Larry Aurie, Mud Bruneteau, Wally Kilrea, Hec Kilrea, Gord Pettinger, Bucko McDonald, Scotty Bowman, Pete Kelly, Doug Young, Ebbie Goodfellow, and Normie Smith. Jack Adams was the general manager and coach, and Honey Walker was the trainer.

 Who was the captain of that team?

 Doug Young, a defenseman. He was born and raised in Medicine Hat, Alberta.

 Hockey players seven decades ago did not make such big salaries. How did Ebbie Goodfellow supplement his income?

 He worked as caddie master at Detroit's Oakland Hills Country Club, and had a job as a tool and die salesman.

One of the smallest men (5' 6" and 148 pounds) in the NHL but one of the toughest, he was called "Little Dempsey" for his fistic skills. He became team captain in 1933, helped the Wings win their first two Cups in 1936 and 1937, and played his entire career in Detroit. Identify him.

Larry Aurie. He was on his way to winning the 1937 scoring title but broke his leg and finished three points behind Sweeney Schriner of the New York Americans. Aurie, who had a knack for killing penalties, was a player-coach in Pittsburgh in 1939. He came back to Detroit for one game in an emergency and scored the winning goal that night—not a bad way to end an NHL career.

Aurie and teammate Herbie Lewis had what honor in 1934?

They represented Detroit in the first NHL All-Star Game, a benefit for Ace Bailey of Toronto, who had been seriously injured in a game with the Bruins.

What is the controversy over Aurie's number being retired?

*The Official NHL Guide and Record Book* had listed it as retired since 1975, at which time the book began featuring retired numbers. Three Detroit numbers were on record as being retired: Aurie's No. 6, Gordie Howe's No. 9, and Alex Delvecchio's No. 10. But before the 2001 season, owner Mike Ilitch ordered the number put back into circulation.

The Red Wings have scored nine goals in a playoff game twice.
When did they achieve this?

Both times it was against the Toronto Maple Leafs—by scores of 9-4
on April 7, 1936, and 9-1 on March 29, 1947.

Sid Howe and Larry Aurie combined to do a rather impressive thing
against the Maple Leafs on November 5, 1936. What was it?

They each scored a goal in a span of seven seconds.

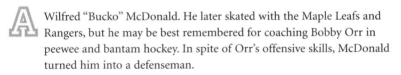

Standing 5' 10" and weighing 205 pounds, he was a steady player
who earned a spot in the Red Wings' lineup from 1936 to 1939.
He scored three goals in the playoffs as Detroit won the 1936 Stanley
Cup. Name him.

Wilfred "Bucko" McDonald. He later skated with the Maple Leafs and
Rangers, but he may be best remembered for coaching Bobby Orr in
peewee and bantam hockey. In spite of Orr's offensive skills, McDonald
turned him into a defenseman.

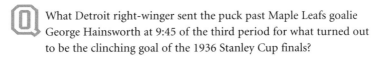

What Detroit right-winger sent the puck past Maple Leafs goalie George Hainsworth at 9:45 of the third period for what turned out to be the clinching goal of the 1936 Stanley Cup finals?

Pete Kelly. "There were no TV cameras then," Kelly recalled many years after the fact. "We didn't parade around the ice with the Cup. It was presented to us later at the Royal York Hotel [in Toronto]. There were quite a few fans from Detroit crowded in there, I remember. April 11, 1936—it was quite a moment."

What was the headline on the front page of the next day's *Detroit Times*?

"The Holy Grail at Last."

The Red Wings won the 1936 Stanley Cup, which might have surprised some fans considering the team's results the year before. How had they done in '35?

Adams' boys finished last in the American Division of the NHL.

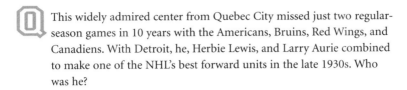

This widely admired center from Quebec City missed just two regular-season games in 10 years with the Americans, Bruins, Red Wings, and Canadiens. With Detroit, he, Herbie Lewis, and Larry Aurie combined to make one of the NHL's best forward units in the late 1930s. Who was he?

Marty Barry, who scored 40 points in 1936 and a career-high 44 the next year. His play was crucial to the franchise's great success during that period. The Wings won the Stanley Cup in both 1936 and 1937, becoming the first American team to capture back-to-back titles. Barry played one final season in Montreal before retiring.

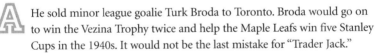

What deal did Adams make after the 1937 season that he soon came to regret?

He sold minor league goalie Turk Broda to Toronto. Broda would go on to win the Vezina Trophy twice and help the Maple Leafs win five Stanley Cups in the 1940s. It would not be the last mistake for "Trader Jack."

This University of Michigan alumnus was with the Red Wings five different times, even though he played just 19 regular-season games. But he managed to hand out an assist in the 1937 Stanley Cup finals against New York. Name him.

John Sherf.

**Q** When all-star goalie Normie Smith suffered an arm injury in the midst of a semifinal series against the Canadiens in 1937, Montreal GM Cecil Hart virtually proclaimed victory. But what minor league call-up saved the day?

**A** Earl Robertson, who made his NHL debut in Game 4 of the best-of-five set against the Habs. Robertson was a 3-1 loser that night but posted a 2-1 win in Game 5, propelling Detroit to the finals. In another five-game series, Robertson had shutouts in Games 4 and 5 to clinch the title over the New York Rangers. Robertson never played another game for the Red Wings, but he spent four good years with the Americans.

**Q** The 1938 season was noted for Detroit's shocking plunge to the cellar of the American Division. Did the two-time defending champs have a single bright moment that year?

**A** Perhaps one—when left-winger Carl Liscombe set a record for the fastest hat trick. Liscombe scored three goals over a span of 1 minute and 52 seconds in a 5-1 win over the Black Hawks. His record has since been broken.

**Q** "Lefty" Liscombe, who came from Perth, Ontario, played nearly 400 games for the Red Wings from 1938 through 1946. What was his peak?

**A** He was a key member of the 1943 Stanley Cup champs and scored 36 goals in 1944 while sharing the line with Syd Howe and Mud Bruneteau. Liscombe was never intimidated, scrapping once with the Maple Leafs' notorious bad guy, Red Horner.

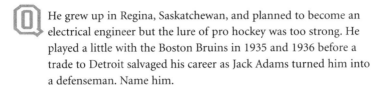

 He grew up in Regina, Saskatchewan, and planned to become an electrical engineer but the lure of pro hockey was too strong. He played a little with the Boston Bruins in 1935 and 1936 before a trade to Detroit salvaged his career as Jack Adams turned him into a defenseman. Name him.

 Alex Motter. He did not favor Adams' move but mastered the new position and stayed with the Wings for six years. In his last year, he helped the team win the 1943 Stanley Cup.

 What goaltender had won the Vezina Trophy four times in Boston before coming to the Red Wings in 1939?

 Cecil "Tiny" Thompson, who was being eased out in Beantown in favor of rookie Frank Brimsek. His arrival in Detroit was seen as a saving grace. Adams pronounced him "the greatest goalie in the world" and the Wings, the league's worst team in 1938, needed all the help they could get. Thompson would stay in Detroit for two years as a stabilizing influence, working behind a young defense. His puckstopping skills allowed the team to overachieve and reach the Stanley Cup semifinals in successive seasons.

How did the Wings get Thompson?

 They sent fellow netminder Normie Smith and $15,000 to Boston. Thompson, by the way, had a brother named Paul who played for Chicago, and they had both been first-team All-Stars in 1938.

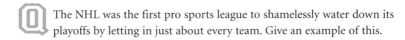

The NHL was the first pro sports league to shamelessly water down its playoffs by letting in just about every team. Give an example of this.

In 1939, seven teams competed in a one-division format. Just one—the defending champion Chicago Black Hawks—did not get to participate in postseason action. The Red Wings, with a none-too-impressive record of 18-24-6, beat the Canadiens (even worse at 15-24-9) in a quarterfinal series and then lost to the Maple Leafs in the semis.

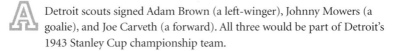

Three amateur players signed with the Wings in one week in October 1939. Who were they?

Detroit scouts signed Adam Brown (a left-winger), Johnny Mowers (a goalie), and Joe Carveth (a forward). All three would be part of Detroit's 1943 Stanley Cup championship team.

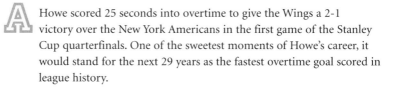

What did Syd Howe do on March 19, 1940?

Howe scored 25 seconds into overtime to give the Wings a 2-1 victory over the New York Americans in the first game of the Stanley Cup quarterfinals. One of the sweetest moments of Howe's career, it would stand for the next 29 years as the fastest overtime goal scored in league history.

The Boston Bruins, led by high-scoring center Bill Cowley, were the class of the league in 1941. They met Detroit in the Stanley Cup finals with what outcome?

 It was a 4-0 sweep for the Bruins.

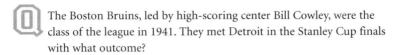 With Don Grosso scoring 52 points, Detroit reached the 1942 Stanley Cup playoffs, beat the Canadiens in the quarters and the Bruins in the semis. How did it go in the finals?

 All was rosy after three games, which were won by the Wings. Then, to their dismay, Toronto won Game 4 on April 12, Game 5 on April 14, Game 6 on April 16, and took the series on April 18 with a 3-1 win at Maple Leaf Gardens. Their comeback from a 3-0 series deficit was the first time such a rally had been achieved in North American professional sports.

 How and why did the Wings lose Game 4 of that series?

 Adams had assaulted official Mel Harwood, earning a suspension. Without him on the bench, the team suffered an infamous collapse.

When the New York Americans folded after the 1942 season, which of their players came to Detroit?

Pat Egan, Murray Armstrong, and Harry Watson.

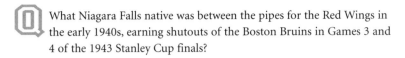

What Niagara Falls native was between the pipes for the Red Wings in the early 1940s, earning shutouts of the Boston Bruins in Games 3 and 4 of the 1943 Stanley Cup finals?

Johnny Mowers. No sooner had that lanky goalie won the Vezina Trophy than he joined the Royal Canadian Air Force to fight in World War II. When he came back, Mowers found that the job had been won by Harry Lumley.

Defenseman Jimmy Orlando, a Red Wing for six years, was adept at the rough stuff, twice going over 100 minutes in penalties and moving to the sin bin. He had a little incident in 1943 during a game against Toronto. What happened?

Orlando got into a stick-swinging fight with Gaye Stewart of the Maple Leafs and came out on the short end, with face cuts and profuse bleeding. Both Orlando and Stewart were suspended.

He scored a hat trick against the Boston Bruins in the first game of the 1943 Stanley Cup finals. Who was he?

Mud Bruneteau.

The New York Rangers paid a visit to the Olympia on January 23, 1944. Who won that game?

Jack Adams' Wings took the 15-0 laugher. Eleven days later, Syd Howe set a modern record of six goals in a game during a 12-2 conquest of the lowly Rangers. It is a record that has been equaled twice but never bettered in more than six decades of play since. Weird things happened in sports during the war years, but a remarkably inept team skated for New York in 1944. They won just six games (out of 50) and gave up 310 goals—another dubious record. The Wings, for their part, lost to Chicago in the semis, four games to one.

Who was Mud Bruneteau's co-captain on the '44 Wings?

Bill "Flash" Hollett. He had been a fixture on Boston's blueline since 1936 (helping the Bruins to Lord Stanley's Cup in 1939) and was acquired in 1944 for Pat Egan. Hollett, an All-Star, could not leverage a contract dispute with Wings' general manager Jack Adams. So following the 1946 season, Hollett opted to leave the NHL and play with teams in lesser leagues.

He came out of Renfrew, Ontario, performed well enough in junior hockey to merit a tryout with the Red Wings, and made his debut at Olympia Stadium in 1945 at the tender age of 19. Name this man who went on to have such a big legacy, both with Detroit and the NHL as a whole.

Ted Lindsay, a fierce competitor in a small package. In the 1950 season, he won the Art Ross Trophy as the league's top scorer and his Red Wings team won the Stanley Cup, as they would three times over the next five years. In his career, Lindsay scored more than 800 points, served as captain for several seasons, and—with Doug Harvey of the Montreal Canadiens—organized the NHL Players' Association.

A native of Saskatoon, Saskatchewan, he made the Red Wings team just after World War II ended and peaked in 1950 with 31 regular-season points and nine more in the playoffs as Detroit won the Cup. Who was he?

 Gerry Couture. He later toiled for Montreal and Chicago.

 They called him "Black Jack," and he was a punishing bodychecker, able to rush with the puck when the need arose. His solid play contributed to Detroit's Stanley Cup wins in 1943 and 1950, and his often-rough style of play led to a reputation as one of the game's bad boys. Identify this native of Pilot Mound, Manitoba.

 Jack Stewart, an outstanding defender during his 12 NHL seasons (10 with Detroit, 2 with Chicago).

 During World War II, Stewart spent a year with the Royal Canadian Air Force. What did he do after returning from the military?

He was back in Detroit, teaming successfully with Bill Quackenbush on defense. In the late 1940s, Stewart waged a running battle with Bruins forward Milt Schmidt. The two often exchanged brutal open-ice hits that the fans couldn't get enough of. Sid Abel, Ted Lindsay, and Gordie Howe often said Stewart deserved more credit for helping make the Red Wings a dominant team.

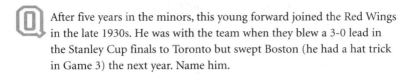

 After five years in the minors, this young forward joined the Red Wings in the late 1930s. He was with the team when they blew a 3-0 lead in the Stanley Cup finals to Toronto but swept Boston (he had a hat trick in Game 3) the next year. Name him.

 Don "the Count" Grosso, who was sent to the Black Hawks early in the 1945 season.

 How did Grosso come by his nickname?

 He had an uncanny resemblance to Bela Lugosi's Dracula.

 Did Gordie Howe win the 1947 Calder Trophy?

He did not. The NHL's top rookie that year was Howie Meeker of Toronto. Meeker, who was with the Leafs in 1956 and 1957, had a rather forgettable career, especially in light of the monumental things Howe would do over a quarter-century.

What Scottish-born forward scored a career-high 24 goals for the Wings in 1944 and later spent five seasons in Chicago?

Adam Brown.

What did Mud Bruneteau do against Boston on March 29, 1945?

 It was the fifth game of the first round of the playoffs, and he scored at 17:12 in overtime to beat the Bruins, 3-2.

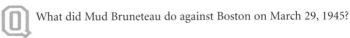

 In a 15-year career, he was one of the best defensemen in the NHL and helped the Rangers and Black Hawks win titles. He came to Detroit at the tail end of his career and played in just 43 games. Identify this native of Kitchener, Ontario.

Earl Seibert, son of pro hockey pioneer Oliver Seibert. He was widely regarded as second only to Eddie Shore in terms of skillful, rugged play, and Shore once admitted that Seibert was the only man he would not fight. Defensively, Seibert was one of the best shot-blockers in the game, and he could move the puck quickly.

 For what else was Seibert known?

Due to a head injury he suffered in the late 1930s, he was one of the first pro hockey players to wear a helmet on a regular basis.

What right-winger, a native of Calgary, scored 38 points for Detroit in 1942, fought for Canada in World War II, and finished his NHL career with the Chicago Black Hawks?

 Eddie Wares.

 What was Wares' role in Detroit's meltdown in the '42 Stanley Cup finals against Toronto?

 The sixth-year right-winger, who had set up the winning goal in the Wings' Game 2 victory, refused to go to the penalty box when ordered to do so by referee Mel Harwood. That precipitated a huge fight, and the winning Leafs were off and running to the championship.

 Who holds the team record for most assists in a game by a defenseman?

 Eddie Bush, who had four against Toronto on April 9, 1942. He had a total of six that entire season. Bush did play quite well for the Wings as they went to seven games with the Maple Leafs before falling.

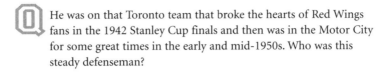

He was on that Toronto team that broke the hearts of Red Wings fans in the 1942 Stanley Cup finals and then was in the Motor City for some great times in the early and mid-1950s. Who was this steady defenseman?

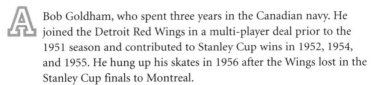

Bob Goldham, who spent three years in the Canadian navy. He joined the Detroit Red Wings in a multi-player deal prior to the 1951 season and contributed to Stanley Cup wins in 1952, 1954, and 1955. He hung up his skates in 1956 after the Wings lost in the Stanley Cup finals to Montreal.

The NHL had been shrinking for 10 years. The Philadelphia Quakers (previously the Pittsburgh Pirates) called it quits in 1932, the St. Louis Eagles (Ottawa Senators) in 1935, the Montreal Maroons in 1938, and the New York Americans in 1942. The remaining teams began to follow baseball's lead by developing farm systems. What else was done to develop future hockey talent?

The league allotted each club the rights to all amateur players within a 50-mile radius. This was good news for Montreal, Toronto, and Detroit—which got many a player from southwestern Ontario. But it was less beneficial to Boston, New York, or Chicago, none of which would win a Stanley Cup between 1942 and 1960.

He was a key element in the Wings' winning the 1943 Stanley Cup, had consecutive 20-goal seasons, and was such a hot commodity that Adams sent him to Boston in '46 for Roy Conacher. Who was this native of Regina, Saskatchewan?

Joe Carveth, who found himself back in Detroit in the middle of the 1950 season. Replacing an injured Gordie Howe, he filled the breach and the Wings won the Cup again. Within a year, Carveth had been demoted to the minors and stayed there for the remainder of his career.

What team record does Carveth still hold?

 Most points scored in one period. On January 23, 1944, he scored four points in one period against the New York Rangers—all on assists.

 The 1945 Red Wings finished in second place but well behind Montreal, clearly the class of the league. Who beat whom in the Stanley Cup playoffs?

 The Canadiens fell in six to the Maple Leafs, and Detroit needed seven (including one in OT) to beat Boston. Toronto won the first three, with goalie Frank McCool getting three shutouts. Then it was Detroit's turn to win three. On April 22, 1945, Toronto got a winning goal from Babe Pratt and took the hardware. This was the first time in the history of Game 7 Stanley Cup finals that the home team failed to win, and it would not happen again until 1971.

 He became known as "boot nose" after Maurice Richard gave him a beating in a game, and was Detroit's captain in 1943 and from 1947 to 1952. Who was this accomplished, playmaking center?

 Sid Abel. In only his second full NHL season, he averaged more than a point per game playing on the "Liniment Line" with Don Grosso and Eddie Wares, and was a second-team All-Star. Abel, who made many contributions to the Wings' Stanley Cup championship run in 1943, missed two seasons doing his bit for the war effort.

What did Abel do after being traded to Chicago in '52?

 The trade was a difficult yet prudent decision for GM Jack Adams since Abel's best years were behind him. Abel went on to be a player-coach in the Windy City for two years. Midway through the 1958 season, he got the Red Wings' coaching job when Jimmy Skinner resigned due to illness. Abel stayed behind the bench for nearly a decade (more than 800 games) and took over as GM when Adams was fired in 1963. Under his guidance, Detroit got to the Stanley Cup finals four times—1961, 1963, 1964, and 1966. Abel would later serve as an executive and/or coach with the Los Angeles Kings, St. Louis Blues, and Kansas City Scouts.

 This man, raised in Regina, Saskatchewan, played 118 games for Detroit from 1944 until halfway through the 1946 season, at which time Jack Adams demoted him in favor of a rookie named Gordie Howe. Who was he?

 Murray Armstrong, later the hockey coach at the University of Denver.

# GRAPHIC

DETROIT FREE PRESS
January 14, 1951

**DETROIT** Red Wings' star forwards, Ted Lindsay (left) and Gordie Howe, team up on and off the ice. (See page 2.)

# TEAMMATES

Terrible Ted (Ted Lindsay) and Mr. Hockey (Gordie Howe)

# CHAPTER THREE
## №. 9

A 15-year-old from Floral, Saskatchewan, managed to get a tryout with the New York Rangers in 1943. Gordie Howe did not make the cut, however. The camp director was unimpressed, telling him, "You're too awkward, son. You'll never make the major leagues." But just three years later, in a tryout with the Red Wings, Jack Adams seemed to like him quite a bit, calling the husky youngster "the best prospect I've seen in 20 years." Howe would score a goal against Toronto in his NHL debut; two games later his legendary mean streak was on display when Black Hawks goalie Paul Bibeault wandered from the net to play the puck and got blasted by the Wings' rook.

Like the very best in other sports—comparisons with Babe Ruth, Muhammad Ali, and Michael Jordan are appropriate—his career can scarcely be encapsulated. Howe, on the right wing, was a great goal scorer and a gifted playmaker who took full advantage of his strength to dominate the opposition. Fans of the Montreal Canadiens might disagree, but Howe soon proved himself the greatest of all hockey players, Maurice Richard included. The 6', 205-pound Howe would lead Detroit to four Stanley Cups (1950, 1952, 1954, and 1955), play in 21 All-Star Games, and did not retire—from the Red Wings, at least—until 1971. Twenty-five years in the NHL—there are reasons why it had never been done before and never since, although his Red Wings teammate Alex Delvecchio came close with 24.

Howe found his new job in the Red Wings front office unfulfilling and soon signed with the Houston Aeros of the new World Hockey Association for the chance to play with his sons Mark and Marty. If he was not the Howe of the early 1950s, he still carried his new team to consecutive championships and was chosen the league's MVP in 1974. With the Hartford/New England Whalers (who had by then joined the NHL), Mr. Hockey was back where he belonged for one final season. In 1979, he participated in all 80 games, scored 15 goals, and played in the All-Star Game as a nod to his storied career. That game, held in Detroit at Joe Louis Arena, featured some thunderous standing ovations for Howe. On April 11, 1980, in his final game (the Whalers lost to Montreal, 4-3), he was 52 years old.

The numbers from the NHL, massive though they are, don't do justice to Howe: 1,850 total points (801 goals and 1,049 assists), 1,756 games played, six times the league's MVP. Howe would become a good friend of Wayne Gretzky, who had idolized him as a young player—and wore No. 99 to honor him—and who later broke some of Howe's scoring records and milestones.

 For what minor league teams did Howe play?

 The Saskatoon Lions, Galt Red Wings, and Omaha Knights.

 Gordie Howe was one of the bigger players in the league, never hesitating to throw his weight around, never backing away from a fight. Give one example from his rookie year.

 In Howe's first game at the Montreal Forum, the Canadiens' Maurice Richard gave him a shove and a few angry words. With a single punch, Howe knocked Richard out cold. He used to say that he played religious hockey—"it is better to give than to receive."

Were Syd Howe and Gordie Howe related?

 They shared a love for hockey, but no DNA.

 Gordie Howe did have a brother who played hockey, however. Who was he?

 Right-winger Vic Howe played parts of three seasons with the New York Rangers (and scored a total of seven points) in the 1950s. The younger brother of the great Gordie, he achieved most of his success in the minors and also played in Europe. After his playing days, Vic Howe spent 30 years as a constable with the Canadian National Railway.

 Who among the Red Wings wore No. 9 in the decade prior to Gordie Howe's arrival in 1947?

 Mud Bruneteau, John Sorrell, Joe Lamb, John Sherf, Connie Brown, Ken Kilrea, Ed Bruneteau, Sid Abel, and Roy Conacher.

 While we're on the topic, who wore No. 7 before Ted Lindsay came along in 1945?

 Marty Barry, Alex Motter, Don Deacon, Sid Abel, Ken Kilrea, and Carl Liscombe. Lindsay's number was not retired until 1991, so 20 more men wore it until then. Tom Bissett was the last.

Alex Delvecchio's No. 10 was retired at the same time as Terrible Ted's—November 10, 1991. Who wore it before him?

 Cliff Purpur, Steve Wochy, Fern Gauthier, Gerry Brown, Gerry Couture, Max McNab, Ed Bruneteau, Jim Peters, and Metro Prystai. Six more Red Wings, the last being Jimmy Carson, would wear No. 10.

 Terry Sawchuk's No. 1 was retired on March 6, 1994. Who wore it in the decade before his arrival in 1950?

 Alf Moore, Claude Bourque, Johnny Mowers, Joe Turner, Connie Dior, Harry Lumley, and Ralph Adams. Glen Hanlon was the last of 17 others to wear it.

 Sid Abel's No. 12 went up to the rafters of Joe Louis Arena on April 29, 1995. Name the Red Wings who wore it in the 10 years before he joined the Wings.

 John Sorrell, Walt Buswell, Hec Kilrea, and Byron McDonald. Thirty-nine others would wear it before the number was retired. Bob Errey was the last.

How many times did Howe have at least 100 penalty minutes?

 Four—1954, 1956, 1963, and 1965.

 As a 17-year-old rookie in 1944, he had a miserable introduction to the NHL, giving up 13 goals in his first two games. But he went on to become one of the league's top goaltenders over a 16-year career that included stints with five of the Original Six teams. Who was this man they called "Apple Cheeks"?

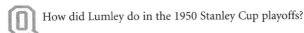 Harry Lumley, out of Owen Sound, Ontario. He was Detroit's backstop when they came within one game of winning the 1945 Stanley Cup. Over the next five years, Lumley—and the Red Wings—were among the league's best in a highly competitive era.

 How did Lumley do in the 1950 Stanley Cup playoffs?

He had three shutouts and a minuscule 1.85 goals-against average, as Detroit overcame the three-time defending champion Toronto Maple Leafs and the New York Rangers. It was Lumley's first and only Stanley Cup. And since Adams was enamored with young Terry Sawchuk, Lumley was expendable. Just a week after hoisting the Cup, Lumley was dealt to the Chicago Black Hawks, the league's worst team.

Center Billy "the Kid" Taylor played just one year with the Red Wings but did set an NHL record on March 16, 1947. What was it?

 Taylor had seven assists in a 10-6 win over the Chicago Black Hawks. A native of Winnipeg, he would later be suspended by league president Clarence Campbell for gambling violations.

 As the Red Wings faced the New York Rangers in the 1948 semis, who was quoted as saying, "In hockey, you have to be mean or you get pushed around"?

 Ted Lindsay. Detroit won that series in six. The finals were between the Red Wings and the Maple Leafs. A close match was expected from the two powerhouses, but Toronto, led by high-scoring center Ted Kennedy, beat Detroit four straight.

 Hubert "Bill" Quackenbush was an excellent defender who relied on precision and discipline rather than brute force during a 14-year NHL career. With Detroit in 1949, he was the first defenseman to win the Lady Byng Trophy. What else did this mild-mannered player do?

 One of hockey's top blueliners, Quackenbush went 131 consecutive games without drawing a penalty. This rather amazing streak had begun in 1948 and did not end until 1950, when he was with the Bruins. He was as popular in Beantown as he had been in Detroit.

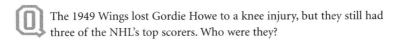 The 1949 Wings lost Gordie Howe to a knee injury, but they still had three of the NHL's top scorers. Who were they?

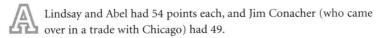 Lindsay and Abel had 54 points each, and Jim Conacher (who came over in a trade with Chicago) had 49.

That Detroit team compiled a 34-19-7 record, best in the league. Did they cruise to an NHL championship?

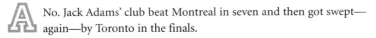 No. Jack Adams' club beat Montreal in seven and then got swept— again—by Toronto in the finals.

How did the Production Line do in 1950?

They finished 1-2-3 in the league scoring parade (the order was Lindsay-Abel-Howe), as the Red Wings won another Stanley Cup.

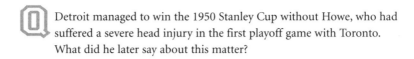 Detroit managed to win the 1950 Stanley Cup without Howe, who had suffered a severe head injury in the first playoff game with Toronto. What did he later say about this matter?

 "I enjoyed my last three Stanley Cups. I don't remember much about the first one."

 What exactly happened to Howe in that game with the Maple Leafs?

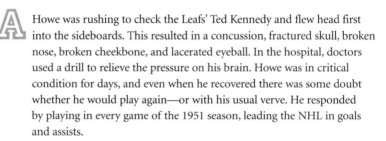 Howe was rushing to check the Leafs' Ted Kennedy and flew head first into the sideboards. This resulted in a concussion, fractured skull, broken nose, broken cheekbone, and lacerated eyeball. In the hospital, doctors used a drill to relieve the pressure on his brain. Howe was in critical condition for days, and even when he recovered there was some doubt whether he would play again—or with his usual verve. He responded by playing in every game of the 1951 season, leading the NHL in goals and assists.

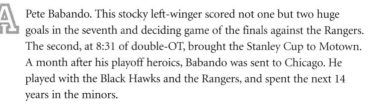 Who scored Detroit's Stanley Cup-winning Game 7 overtime goal in 1950?

Pete Babando. This stocky left-winger scored not one but two huge goals in the seventh and deciding game of the finals against the Rangers. The second, at 8:31 of double-OT, brought the Stanley Cup to Motown. A month after his playoff heroics, Babando was sent to Chicago. He played with the Black Hawks and the Rangers, and spent the next 14 years in the minors.

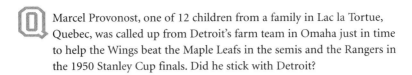 Marcel Provonost, one of 12 children from a family in Lac la Tortue, Quebec, was called up from Detroit's farm team in Omaha just in time to help the Wings beat the Maple Leafs in the semis and the Rangers in the 1950 Stanley Cup finals. Did he stick with Detroit?

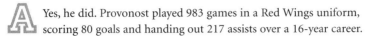 Yes, he did. Provonost played 983 games in a Red Wings uniform, scoring 80 goals and handing out 217 assists over a 16-year career.

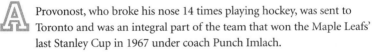 Provonost's name is engraved on the Stanley Cup five times. Four titles were with Detroit. Where did he win his fifth?

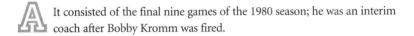 Provonost, who broke his nose 14 times playing hockey, was sent to Toronto and was an integral part of the team that won the Maple Leafs' last Stanley Cup in 1967 under coach Punch Imlach.

How long did Provonost's coaching career last?

It consisted of the final nine games of the 1980 season; he was an interim coach after Bobby Kromm was fired.

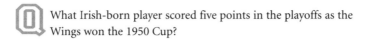 What Irish-born player scored five points in the playoffs as the Wings won the 1950 Cup?

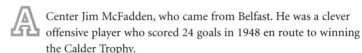 Center Jim McFadden, who came from Belfast. He was a clever offensive player who scored 24 goals in 1948 en route to winning the Calder Trophy.

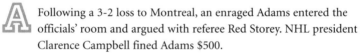 What trouble did Detroit GM Jack Adams get himself into on January 18, 1953?

Following a 3-2 loss to Montreal, an enraged Adams entered the officials' room and argued with referee Red Storey. NHL president Clarence Campbell fined Adams $500.

His NHL career consisted of two stints each with Chicago and Detroit, spanning 1948 to 1958. Just 5' 8" and 155 pounds, he could skate like a gazelle around the rink from his center ice spot. Name this native of Yorkton, Saskatchewan.

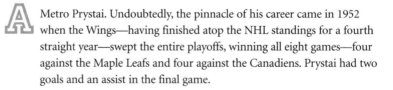 Metro Prystai. Undoubtedly, the pinnacle of his career came in 1952 when the Wings—having finished atop the NHL standings for a fourth straight year—swept the entire playoffs, winning all eight games—four against the Maple Leafs and four against the Canadiens. Prystai had two goals and an assist in the final game.

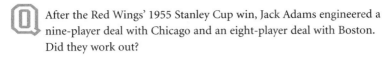 After the Red Wings' 1955 Stanley Cup win, Jack Adams engineered a nine-player deal with Chicago and an eight-player deal with Boston. Did they work out?

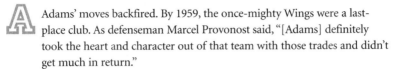 Adams' moves backfired. By 1959, the once-mighty Wings were a last-place club. As defenseman Marcel Provonost said, "[Adams] definitely took the heart and character out of that team with those trades and didn't get much in return."

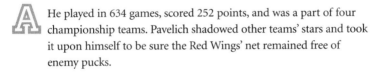 Left-winger Marty Pavelich was one of the fastest players in the game, darting up and down the ice to the amazement and pleasure of onlookers. How did he do in his decade (1948–1957) with the Wings?

He played in 634 games, scored 252 points, and was a part of four championship teams. Pavelich shadowed other teams' stars and took it upon himself to be sure the Red Wings' net remained free of enemy pucks.

How and why did Pavelich's Detroit career end so suddenly?

 Pavelich's friend and business partner, Ted Lindsay, was banished to Chicago in 1957 as retribution for his union activities. Lindsay made the mistake of saying publicly that Pavelich would continue to look after their business interests. Jack Adams was not pleased to hear news that the two Wings had prospects outside of hockey. Rather than get shipped to the minors, Pavelich decided to retire.

 The Detroit Red Wings had been part of the NHL since 1926, but they never had a scoring leader until 1950. Who won the Art Ross Trophy (instituted in 1948), and what other Wings have won it since?

 Ted Lindsay got that honor in 1950 when he scored 78 points. He has been followed only by Gordie Howe (86 points in 1951; 86 points in 1952; 95 points in 1953; 81 points in 1954; 89 points in 1957; 86 points in 1963). There have been many other high-scoring Red Wings since '63, but none led the league.

Alex Delvecchio takes aim in a game against the
Toronto Maple Leafs. Goalie Ed Chadwick defends.

# CHAPTER FOUR
# HOCKEYTOWN

Jack Adams had worn two hats—coach and general manager—virtually since he was hired in Detroit in the late 1920s. Finally, in 1947 he gave up coaching and carried on as the team's GM. The man chosen to replace him on the bench had no NHL experience, but it turned out to be a very astute move. Tommy Ivan would be the Red Wings' coach for eight seasons, during which time they would win three Stanley Cups. Before he retired, he would have one more—as GM of the Chicago Black Hawks.

Yes, the Detroit Red Wings were on the verge of a most impressive run of success. They had Gordie Howe, not yet in his prime but already showing signs of being among the best ever, plus Ted Lindsay, Sid Abel, Red Kelly, Alex Delvecchio, Marcel Provonost, Terry Sawchuk in goal, and other fine players. Ivan's Wings lost to Toronto in the 1948 and 1949 finals before repeatedly scaling the mountain. They beat the New York Rangers in a closely fought seven-game series, following that up with wins over the Montreal Canadiens in 1952, 1954, and 1955.

Do four Cups in a six-year span constitute a dynasty? At the very least, one can count those Red Wings teams as among the best in league history, along with the Ottawa Senators of the 1920s, the Toronto Maple Leafs of 1947–1951, the Canadiens of 1957–1960, the Leafs again from 1962 to 1967, Montreal again in the late 1960s and late 1970s, the New York Islanders of the early 1980s, and Wayne Gretzky's Edmonton Oilers of the late 1980s. Different teams in different eras, but each is deserving of respect and remembrance.

It was not all sweetness and light for the Detroit hockey club in those days. James Norris, Sr., died, setting off an unsavory power struggle between his children over ownership of the team. They finished in the cellar in 1959, and Adams was forced out three years later, although everyone agreed to call it a "retirement." With Abel behind the bench, the Wings were again near the top, making the Stanley Cup finals four times from 1961 to 1966.

In what seasons did Detroit goalie Terry Sawchuk participate in the NHL All-Star Game?

 Each year from 1950 to 1954, and again in 1959 and 1963.

 What was the result of the 1950 NHL All-Star Game?

The game was played at the Olympia, as the host Red Wings took on a team made up of the best of the rest. Still, Detroit had an easy time of it, with a 7-1 victory. It was the first All-Star Game to be televised.

In 1951, the Red Wings sent George Gee, Clare Martin, Jim McFadden, Max McNab, Jim Peters, and Clare Raglan to Chicago. What did they get in return?

$75,000.

Benny Woit, a native of Fort William, Ontario, did his apprenticeship in the minors before getting called up to Detroit in 1951. Woit became a regular on the Wings' blueline, and although the flashier players scored goals and excited fans, he held the fort with his rugged stay-at-home defensive play. He would help the team secure Stanley Cups in 1952, 1954, and 1955. Woit was traded to the Black Hawks following the latter season but never produced as he had with the Red Wings. In 334 NHL games, how much did Benny Woit score?

 He recorded 7 goals and 26 assists for 33 points.

 Identify Pete and Jerry Cusimano.

 These two brothers helped run the family fish store on Detroit's east side. Somehow, they decided that it would bring the Red Wings good luck in the upcoming NHL playoffs to throw a boiled octopus on the ice at Olympia Stadium. An octopus has eight legs, and eight wins (two best-of-seven series) were all a team needed then to win the Stanley Cup. The Cusimanos tossed the ungainly cephalopod over the glass on April 15, 1952, during the Red Wings' Stanley Cup playoff run. Perhaps because the Red Wings swept the series that year, the octopus has been a good luck charm now for more than half a century. No other pro sports franchise has such a whimsical and wacky tradition.

 What is the Red Wings' longest winning streak?

 Nine games, and it has been done five times—in 1951, 1955, 1995, 1996, and 2005.

And the longest losing streak?

 Fourteen games, in 1982. However, the 1977 Detroit team had a woeful stretch of 18 losses and one tie.

 The Original Six era was from 1943 to 1967. How many times did the Red Wings miss the playoffs during that time?

Just three: 1959, 1962, and 1967.

What were the home rinks of the Original Six teams?

The Montreal Forum (which opened in 1924), Madison Square Garden (1925), Detroit Olympia (1927), Boston Garden (1928), Chicago Stadium (1929), and Maple Leaf Gardens (1931). All of them, to varying degrees, were hockey shrines.

From February 11, 1950 (against Boston), until January 29, 1953 (against Toronto), Gordie Howe scored nine hat tricks. Only once during that span did a teammate record one. Who was he?

 Center George Gee did it against Chicago on March 11, 1951.

 He was an accomplished two-way player who could score goals and rub his opponents the wrong way. He was with Detroit in the early 1950s (with some trips to the minors) and early 1960s but saw his greatest success as a Boston Bruin. Name him.

 Vic Stasiuk. A native of Lethbridge, Alberta, he later coached the Philadelphia Flyers, the California Golden Seals, and the Vancouver Canucks.

 How influential was James Norris, Sr., in the NHL?

 At one point, he effectively owned the Chicago Black Hawks, was the largest stockholder in the New York Rangers, and had significant influence over the Boston Bruins due to loans made to the franchise to help keep it alive during the Depression.

What were the roles of Norris' children with the team before and
after his death in 1952?

James Norris, Jr. worked with his father in the 1930s and early 1940s,
signing such future stars as Gordie Howe, Sid Abel, and Red Kelly. In
1946, he and Arthur Wirtz (the senior Norris' original partner in buying
the Red Wings) acquired the Black Hawks and held the team through its
1961 Stanley Cup victory. Marguerite Norris took control of the Red
Wings after their father's death. She was the second female chief executive
in NHL history and the first to have her name engraved on the Stanley
Cup. Marguerite, who detested Jack Adams but kept him on as the Red
Wings' GM, was club president from 1952 to 1955. At that time, her
younger brother Bruce wrested the franchise away and held it until
selling to Mike Ilitch in 1982.

 How did goalie Terry Sawchuk do in the 1952 playoffs?

He turned in one of the best performances in the league's history,
allowing only five goals in eight games. Sawchuk also had four shutouts
at the Olympia for the champion Red Wings.

 How many shutouts did Sawchuk have for the Wings between
1951 and 1955?

No fewer than 56. He was a great goalie, playing on a great team—
an excellent combination.

Sawchuk, considered by some to be hockey's greatest goaltender, won 447 games and recorded 103 shutouts over a 21-year NHL career. And yet the Red Wings traded him twice. For whom else did he play?

 The Boston Bruins, the Toronto Maple Leafs (he helped them win the 1967 Cup), the Los Angeles Kings, and the New York Rangers. Sawchuk, who played most of his career without benefit of a mask, took a lot of pucks to the face, which led to some 600 stitches. A man who struggled with depression and alcohol abuse, he died a mysterious death. In a drunken fight with Rangers teammate Ron Stewart, Sawchuk suffered a lacerated liver and a resulting blood clot stopped his heart on May 31, 1970. He was only 40 years old.

 How did the first round of the 1952 playoffs conclude?

 Lindsay and Howe had received death threats intended to prevent them from playing in Game 4 against Toronto. Needless to say, they played, and Detroit won to end the series. Lindsay then skated out to center ice, wielded his hockey stick like a machine gun and pretended to shoot the Maple Leafs fans.

 He was born in Ireland but grew up in Montreal, fought in World War II, and came back to win a Stanley Cup with the Canadiens. As if that were not enough, he won two more (1950 and 1954) in Detroit. His son of the same name later played for the Wings. So who is he?

 Jim Peters, Sr. His son, Jim, Jr., was a wandering journeyman who appeared in 54 games for Detroit from 1965 to 1968.

Identify Budd Lynch. Hint: He has a rich, baritone voice.

 A native of Windsor, Lynch joined the Canadian Armed Forces during World War II and lost his right arm in combat. Upon his return home, he was the Windsor Spitfires' radio announcer in 1949. Since Jack Adams liked his work, he asked Lynch to move across the river and call the games for his organization. Detroit won the Stanley Cup four times during his first five years with the club. He tried to retire in 1975 but Alex Delvecchio brought him back as director of publicity. Another retirement attempt seven years later failed when Marian Ilitch convinced Lynch to stay on at his current position of public-address announcer at Joe Louis Arena.

 Detroit had but a single penalty shot in the decade of the 1950s. Who took it?

 Gordie Howe, against goalie Gump Worsley of the New York Rangers on May 5, 1953. The Wings had not had a penalty shot since the 1948 season and would not have another until 1962.

 This native of Stoney Creek, Ontario, helped the Wings win two Stanley Cups in the early 1950s. Just a few years earlier, he had become part of the NHL's first-ever father-son duo (his father had been with the New York Americans in the late 1920s). Name him.

 Leo Reise, Jr. He still holds the Red Wings record for most overtime goals in one year's playoffs—two in 1950.

This native of Noranda, Quebec, made a slow ascent to the NHL, finally catching on as a full-time Red Wing in 1952. He established himself as a durable foot soldier, playing in 580 consecutive games over the next decade, thus earning the nickname "Ironman." Identify him.

 Johnny Wilson. He savored three Stanley Cup victories with the Wings before joining the Chicago Black Hawks from 1955 to 1957. He was back with the Wings for two more seasons before finishing with the Leafs and Rangers.

 What distinction do Wilson and his brother Larry hold in Red Wings history?

 They are the only set of brothers to have served as coach of the team: Johnny in parts of 1972 and 1973, and Larry for the last 36 games of the 1977 season.

 In the next 14 years, Johnny Wilson became a very well-traveled coach. How many stops did he have?

 No fewer than 14: the Ottawa Montagnards senior club, Princeton University, Springfield Indians, Los Angeles Kings, Tidewater Sharks, Detroit Red Wings, Indianapolis Racers, Michigan Stags, Baltimore Blades, Cleveland Crusaders, Minnesota Fighting Saints, Colorado Rockies, Team Canada, and Pittsburgh Penguins.

On February 2, 1954, the Red Wings played what has been called the most unique hockey exhibition of all time. Of what did it consist?

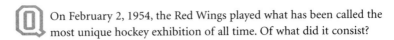 Coach and GM Jack Adams agreed to take his powerhouse Detroit Red Wings (two months away from winning their third Stanley Cup in five years) to the wilds of Michigan's Upper Peninsula to play a team of inmates at Marquette Prison. The brainchild of the prison's recreation director Leonard "Oakie" Brumm, the game was played on the outdoor ice rink Brumm and a group of inmates built in a corner of the prison yard.

 Who won?

 The Red Wings were up, 18-0, at the end of the first period—and they were being charitable. At that point, the teams swapped players and they quit keeping score. All 600 of the prison population (less those in solitary confinement) watched, amazed by the Wings' graceful skating, pinpoint passing, and crisp shots. Adams, Howe, Lindsay, and the others later shared a meal with their hosts and donated some equipment. It never happened again, but all of the Wings recalled that game fondly in the years to come.

 How many shutouts did the 1954 Wings have?

 Thirteen, still a team record. They failed to record any shutouts in 1981, 1982, 1985, and 2006.

Identify the first winner of the Norris Trophy.

 The Red Wings' Leonard "Red" Kelly in 1954. Other Detroit winners have been Paul Coffey (1995) and Nicklas Lidstrom (2001, 2002, 2003, and 2006).

 What other honors did Kelly achieve in his career?

 He won the Lady Byng Trophy four times, served as captain of the Wings from 1956 to 1958, was a member of Canada's Parliament for four years, won a Stanley Cup with Toronto, and coached the Kings, Penguins, and Maple Leafs. In Kelly's 12 years with Detroit, the team won eight regular-season championships and four Stanley Cups, and he was chosen as a first-team All-Star six times. Not bad for a guy who a Toronto scout once predicted would never make it in the NHL.

 He was born in Selkirk, Manitoba, and was the Red Wings' coach in 1955 when they beat Montreal for the Cup. Identify him.

 Jimmy Skinner, who never played in the NHL. He was in a tough spot, since the defending champion Wings were a complacent club that started slowly. But they jelled and closed fast, winning their last nine games. Skinner would accept no credit for the team's success: "It scares me to think of all the mistakes I made, right up to the end. I've been plain lucky."

With whom did Skinner joust in one game that season?

He barked at NHL president Clarence Campbell during a game when the latter complained about the Red Wings using improper language. Skinner would compile a coaching record of 123-78-46 and later serve three seasons as Detroit's GM in the early 1980s.

On December 2, 1954, the Canadiens beat the Red Wings, 4-1, at the Olympia. What else happened?

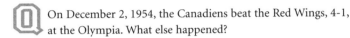

Maurice "Rocket" Richard scored the 398th goal of his career and received a misconduct penalty after arguing with referee Bill Chadwick. In the final two minutes of the game, a free-for-all erupted in front of the Detroit bench and both teams had to be sent to their dressing rooms to cool off. Red Wings coach Jimmy Skinner swapped punches with the Habs' big Butch Bouchard during the melee.

Earl "Dutch" Reibel moved smartly up the ladder of minor league hockey, joining the Red Wings in the 1954 season. Reibel fit right in with Gordie Howe and Ted Lindsay, scoring 70 goals in his first four years. Detroit won two championships while he was there. For what else is Reibel known?

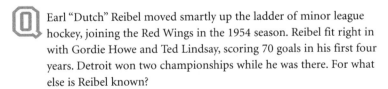

He scored two goals in the 1955 NHL All-Star Game and won the 1956 Lady Byng Trophy. The next year, however, the Wings shipped him to Chicago, and his numbers plummeted. Reibel had savored the Wings' special sense of fidelity, but when those ties were cut, he seemed to lose his zeal. He played out the string with the Black Hawks and Bruins before quitting.

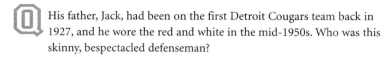 His father, Jack, had been on the first Detroit Cougars team back in 1927, and he wore the red and white in the mid-1950s. Who was this skinny, bespectacled defenseman?

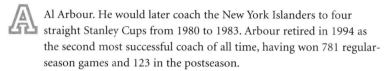 Al Arbour. He would later coach the New York Islanders to four straight Stanley Cups from 1980 to 1983. Arbour retired in 1994 as the second most successful coach of all time, having won 781 regular-season games and 123 in the postseason.

 This defenseman took part in almost 800 games in the NHL from 1953 to 1968. He was a Bruin but left Beantown in the big trade that involved goalie Terry Sawchuk. Name him.

Warren Godfrey, best known as a stabilizing force on the blueline with the Wings.

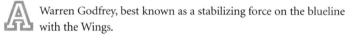

Who, in Detroit Red Wings lore, is known as "Mighty Mouse"?

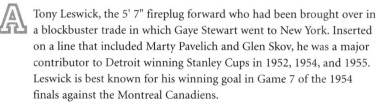 Tony Leswick, the 5' 7" fireplug forward who had been brought over in a blockbuster trade in which Gaye Stewart went to New York. Inserted on a line that included Marty Pavelich and Glen Skov, he was a major contributor to Detroit winning Stanley Cups in 1952, 1954, and 1955. Leswick is best known for his winning goal in Game 7 of the 1954 finals against the Montreal Canadiens.

Name the Wings rookie who, in 1954, scored 17 goals and had eight assists.

 Bill Dineen. He played six NHL seasons but is probably better remembered for his coaching exploits later in life. He coached the Houston Aeros (winning two WHA titles, thanks to the elder Howe), Hartford Whalers, and Philadelphia Flyers. Dineen was the father of four sons (Gary, Gord, Peter, and Kevin) who also made it to the NHL.

 What was "the Richard Riot"?

 The incident happened on March 17, 1955, but it stemmed from a game four days earlier between Montreal and Boston. Maurice Richard, one of the most prolific scorers in hockey, was also the most hot-tempered player on the Flying Frenchmen team. He had fought a Bruin, punched a ref, and got suspended by NHL president Clarence Campbell for the rest of the '55 season and the playoffs. In attendance at the Red Wings–Canadiens game at the Montreal Forum, Campbell was subjected to a torrent of abuse; a minor riot blew up inside the building and then moved outside when the game was forfeited to Detroit. An incensed crowd of 10,000 took to the streets, damaged fashionable stores, upended cars, and set fires. It went on for seven hours before the *gendarmes* got things under control. The visiting Red Wings hunkered down in their locker room during most of the proceedings.

What was the on-ice result of *l'affaire Richard*?

The Rocket-less Canadiens met the Red Wings in the Stanley Cup finals, playing valiantly but losing in seven games.

Name the two Wings who appeared on the cover of *Sports Illustrated* in March 1957.

 Gordie Howe and Ted Lindsay.

 What did the Red Wings give up to get Terry Sawchuk back from the Bruins in 1957?

 They parted with some cash and John Bucyk, who had scored 30 points in two seasons. "The Chief," as he was known, was a skilled left-winger who stood 6', 215 pounds. Bucyk went on to play for two decades in Boston. This native of Edmonton was a member of the so-called Uke Line in Boston with fellow Ukrainian-Canadians Bronco Horvath and Vic Stasiuk. He set a number of Bruins records—including most seasons (21), games (1,436), goals (545), assists (794), and points (1,339).

 How and why did Ted Lindsay leave Detroit?

 In 1957, the first NHL Players' Association had been formed with Lindsay as president. Before long, the owners had crushed the organization and the Red Wings had sent Lindsay to the last-place Chicago Black Hawks.

What happened in the first meeting between Chicago and Detroit after Lindsay was banished?

 Lindsay whacked Gordie Howe with his stick, and his old teammate responded with a punch that felled Lindsay. It should be noted that these two men had been virtually inseparable for 10 years. When Lindsay married in the early 1950s, Howe moved in with the newlyweds.

 This 5' 7" center was in the Red Wings' lineup in 1957 for 69 regular season games, getting 15 goals and 15 assists. He was soon gone to Chicago and the minors but found himself back in Detroit nearly a decade later. Who was he?

 Billy Dea. He also served as the Wings' de facto coach for most of the 1976 and 1977 seasons. Technically, the coach was Alex Delvecchio during those times, but Dea worked behind the bench. He also took over in the final 11 games of the 1982 season when Wayne Maxner was canned.

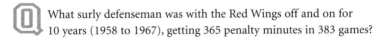

 What surly defenseman was with the Red Wings off and on for 10 years (1958 to 1967), getting 365 penalty minutes in 383 games?

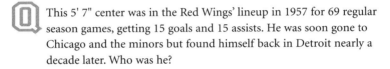 Pete Goegan, who worked hard to get to the NHL and was just about always fighting to keep his job. His life was a revolving door between the Wings, the minors, and other NHL teams. In 1962, Goegan was traded to the Rangers and then sent back to Detroit—for the same player.

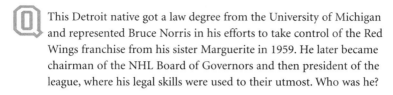

This Detroit native got a law degree from the University of Michigan and represented Bruce Norris in his efforts to take control of the Red Wings franchise from his sister Marguerite in 1959. He later became chairman of the NHL Board of Governors and then president of the league, where his legal skills were used to their utmost. Who was he?

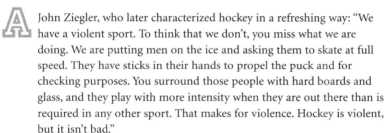

John Ziegler, who later characterized hockey in a refreshing way: "We have a violent sport. To think that we don't, you miss what we are doing. We are putting men on the ice and asking them to skate at full speed. They have sticks in their hands to propel the puck and for checking purposes. You surround those people with hard boards and glass, and they play with more intensity when they are out there than is required in any other sport. That makes for violence. Hockey is violent, but it isn't bad."

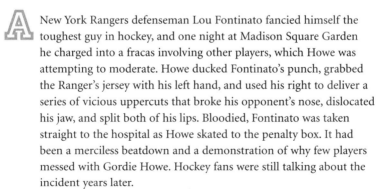

Howe had proven himself a person not to be trifled with early in his career, so much so that he seldom had to fight later on. But he had a memorable tussle on February 1, 1959. What was it?

New York Rangers defenseman Lou Fontinato fancied himself the toughest guy in hockey, and one night at Madison Square Garden he charged into a fracas involving other players, which Howe was attempting to moderate. Howe ducked Fontinato's punch, grabbed the Ranger's jersey with his left hand, and used his right to deliver a series of vicious uppercuts that broke his opponent's nose, dislocated his jaw, and split both of his lips. Bloodied, Fontinato was taken straight to the hospital as Howe skated to the penalty box. It had been a merciless beatdown and a demonstration of why few players messed with Gordie Howe. Hockey fans were still talking about the incident years later.

 How did the Detroit Red Wings Alumni Association come into existence?

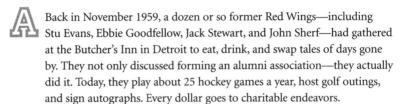 Back in November 1959, a dozen or so former Red Wings—including Stu Evans, Ebbie Goodfellow, Jack Stewart, and John Sherf—had gathered at the Butcher's Inn in Detroit to eat, drink, and swap tales of days gone by. They not only discussed forming an alumni association—they actually did it. Today, they play about 25 hockey games a year, host golf outings, and sign autographs. Every dollar goes to charitable endeavors.

Besides being linemates, what did Detroit's Glen Skov and Marty Pavelich have in common?

They had brothers who worked in striped shirts: Art Skov was a referee, and Matt Pavelich was a linesman.

This left-winger was a solid two-way player, well-respected by teammates and opponents. With 28 minutes in the penalty box in an NHL career lasting 820 games (1959–1972), he was also among the cleanest players in hockey. Identify him.

Val Fonteyne, a native of Wetaskiwin, Alberta. He played a total of seven years in Motown and helped the team reach the 1961, 1963, and 1966 Stanley Cup finals. Fonteyne was not on the Detroit team that also reached the 1964 finals, at which time he was with the Rangers.

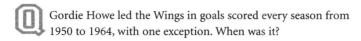 Gordie Howe led the Wings in goals scored every season from 1950 to 1964, with one exception. When was it?

 In 1961, when center Norm Ullman was the team's top goal scorer, with 28.

 He was a steady pivot for Detroit for most of four years, helping the team reach the 1961 Stanley Cup finals. But the next season, coach Sid Abel sent him to the minors and then traded him to Chicago. Identify this native of Campbell River, British Columbia.

Len Lunde.

On December 16, 1962, Detroit and New York met at Madison Square Garden. The Rangers won, 5-2, but the game was spoiled by a brawl. Who were the chief participants?

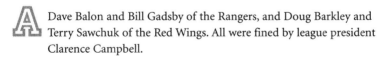 Dave Balon and Bill Gadsby of the Rangers, and Doug Barkley and Terry Sawchuk of the Red Wings. All were fined by league president Clarence Campbell.

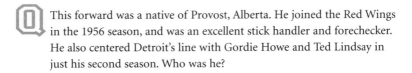 This forward was a native of Provost, Alberta. He joined the Red Wings in the 1956 season, and was an excellent stick handler and forechecker. He also centered Detroit's line with Gordie Howe and Ted Lindsay in just his second season. Who was he?

Norm Ullman. With 490 career regular-season goals and 739 assists, he ranks among the greatest centers to ever play in the NHL. Ullman led Detroit in goals in 1961, 1965, and 1966. During his 20-year career, he scored 30 goals and added 53 assists in 106 Stanley Cup playoff games, although he never was on a winner. On March 3, 1968, while in his 13th season with Detroit, Ullman, Paul Henderson, and Floyd Smith were traded to Toronto for Frank Mahovlich, Pete Stemkowski, Garry Unger, and the rights to Carl Brewer. Ullman finished his NHL career with the Maple Leafs and then played two seasons with the Edmonton Oilers of the WHA.

 What team record did Ullman set in 1963 (which he tied in '64)?

He had five points in a playoff game—both times against Chicago. Steve Yzerman would tie the record in a game against St. Louis in 1996.

 The NHL's first amateur draft was in 1963. Who did Detroit take in the first round that year?

Pete Mahovlich, a member of the team from 1966 to 1969. Brother of Frank Mahovlich, he was known as "Little M" and probably had his best years with the Canadiens and Penguins. In his 16-year NHL career, Mahovlich had 288 goals and 485 assists for 773 points in 884 games.

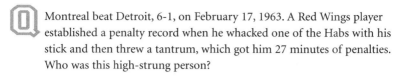

 Montreal beat Detroit, 6-1, on February 17, 1963. A Red Wings player established a penalty record when he whacked one of the Habs with his stick and then threw a tantrum, which got him 27 minutes of penalties. Who was this high-strung person?

 Defenseman Howie Young, who also got a three-game suspension.

 Bruce MacGregor was a model of consistency for the Wings from 1961 until 1971. What was his best year as a scorer?

He scored 28 goals for the 1965 Wings. MacGregor later spent four years with the Rangers and was an assistant GM with the Oilers.

The scouts so admired this Calgary native that the Black Hawks gave him a $3,000 signing bonus and a salary of $7,500. And he was with the team after just 12 minor league games. He played in the Windy City for the better part of nine seasons, then six with the New York Rangers before coming over to Detroit. Name this man who, like Terry Sawchuk, was reputed to have received 600 stitches to his face in an NHL career that stretched from 1946 to 1966.

Bill Gadsby, and 12 of those stitches came in his first game with Chicago. Always a star in the league, he played 1,248 regular-season games but only 67 playoff games. His teams made it to the finals thrice but never won.

Shortly after retiring, Gadsby was named head coach of the Red Wings. How did he do while behind the bench?

He was there in 1969 and the first two games of the '70 season before being asked to depart the premises. Gadsby's record was 35-31-12.

Name the left-winger who shuttled between the New York Rangers and the minor leagues for four years before a trade to Detroit in 1961 allowed him to show his stuff. Hint: In the 1963 season, he scored 33 goals, eight of them game-winners.

Parker MacDonald, who later coached the Minnesota North Stars and Los Angeles Kings, although without great success.

Right-winger Floyd Smith, who spent nearly a decade in the minors, had a fairly undistinguished playing career with the Rangers, Red Wings (1963–1968), and Sabres. For what is he better known?

Smith was a coach with Buffalo—guiding the team to the 1975 Stanley Cup finals—and Toronto. He was later the Leafs' general manager.

This speedy right-winger took part in 33 playoff games with the Wings from 1964 to 1966. Then, after being traded to the defending Stanley Cup-champion Toronto Maple Leafs, he was in just 19 over seven seasons. Name him.

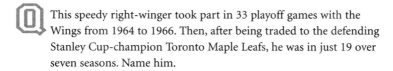 Paul Henderson, who is best known for scoring what some hockey writers called "the goal of the century" in 1972 as Team Canada clinched the Summit Series against the USSR in the dying seconds of the eighth and final game.

 Between 1957 and 1965, this tricky right-winger shuttled between Detroit and the Wings' minor league affiliate in Edmonton no fewer than five times. Who was he?

Billy McNeill, a role player who took part in the Stanley Cup playoffs for the only time in his career in 1958. Two years later, he was traded to the New York Rangers with Red Kelly for Eddie Shack and Bill Gadsby. McNeill made headlines with his refusal to report—a gutsy move for a man who lacked a major reputation.

This defenseman, a native of Regina, Saskatchewan, had an 18-year career that included stints in Montreal, Los Angeles, Detroit, St. Louis, and Colorado. He served as captain of the Kings and Wings, and won five Stanley Cups with the Canadiens. Name him.

 Terry Harper.

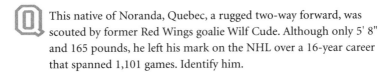

This native of Noranda, Quebec, a rugged two-way forward, was scouted by former Red Wings goalie Wilf Cude. Although only 5' 8" and 165 pounds, he left his mark on the NHL over a 16-year career that spanned 1,101 games. Identify him.

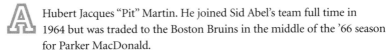

Hubert Jacques "Pit" Martin. He joined Sid Abel's team full time in 1964 but was traded to the Boston Bruins in the middle of the '66 season for Parker MacDonald.

When did Gordie Howe break the scoring record of his old nemesis, Maurice Richard?

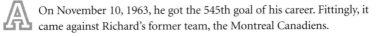

On November 10, 1963, he got the 545th goal of his career. Fittingly, it came against Richard's former team, the Montreal Canadiens.

Who holds the franchise record for most playoff penalty minutes in his career?

Gordie Howe, with 218.

 Did Howe ever lead the Red Wings in penalty minutes?

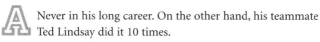 Never in his long career. On the other hand, his teammate
Ted Lindsay did it 10 times.

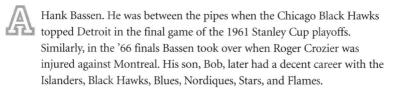 This goalie was nicknamed "Mr. Emergency" because he was usually not
the top guy, whether in Detroit (1961–1967) or elsewhere. Who was he?

Hank Bassen. He was between the pipes when the Chicago Black Hawks
topped Detroit in the final game of the 1961 Stanley Cup playoffs.
Similarly, in the '66 finals Bassen took over when Roger Crozier was
injured against Montreal. His son, Bob, later had a decent career with the
Islanders, Black Hawks, Blues, Nordiques, Stars, and Flames.

 The Lester Patrick Trophy is given for outstanding service to American
hockey. Name the Red Wings who have won it.

Jack Adams in 1966, Gordie Howe in 1967, Alex Delvecchio in 1974,
Bruce Norris in 1975, Mike Ilitch in 1991, and Scotty Bowman in 2001.

He was a member of the Red Wings from 1969 until 1971, but he is best remembered for something he did *to* them in the 1964 Stanley Cup playoffs. Who was he, and what did he do?

 The man in question is Bob Baun, who had a 17-year NHL career, most of it with Toronto. In Game 6 of the 1964 finals, he was hit in the foot by one of Gordie Howe's shots, which broke his ankle. Baun was carried by stretcher off the ice; he took a painkilling shot, laced his skates back up, and returned. Two minutes into overtime, his deflected shot went by Terry Sawchuk to win. The irrepressible Baun also played two nights later when the Leafs wrapped up the title.

 This defenseman, while property of the talent-rich Montreal Canadiens, was stuck behind many others. But when Detroit claimed him during the 1964 NHL intra-league draft, he jumped right into the Wings' lineup and stayed there for a decade. Who was he?

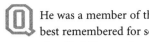 Gary Bergman.

What incident is Bergman remembered for during his rookie season?

 He got tangled up with Montreal's Henri Richard when Richard scored the Stanley Cup-winning goal against the Wings in overtime during Game 6 of the 1966 finals. Bergman, and many others, believed Richard gave the puck an illegal nudge with his glove.

 Hailing from Bracebridge, Ontario, goalie Roger Crozier is, rather amazingly, the most recent of Red Wings to win the Calder Trophy—back in 1965. How did he do that year?

Crozier started all 70 games, leading the league with 40 wins and 6 shutouts. The next season, he and the Red Wings made it to the Stanley Cup finals against Montreal. Although Detroit lost that six-game series, Crozier's efforts in net earned him the Conn Smythe Trophy as Stanley Cup playoffs MVP. The first player to win the Conn Smythe in a losing effort, Crozier was traded to Buffalo in 1970.

Besides Crozier, which Detroit players have won the Conn Smythe Trophy?

 Mike Vernon (1997), Steve Yzerman (1998), and Nicklas Lidstrom (2002).

 How was Crozier honored by the league in 2000?

 That year, the NHL unveiled the Roger Crozier Award. It is given annually to the goalie with the best save percentage.

 What familiar face was back with the Wings for the '65 season?

 Ted Lindsay, then 39 years of age. He had played three years in Chicago and retired in 1961. He came back when asked by his old buddy, coach and general manager Sid Abel. Lindsay proved he could still play, helping the Red Wings win their first regular-season title in seven years. Only then, after 1,201 games, did his playing career end.

Bryan Watson, who grew up in a mining town in northern Ontario, was with the Red Wings for two seasons in the 1960s and four in the 1970s. For what is he best known?

 Watson, small in stature but always willing to tussle, was an average skater at best with little scoring touch around the net. But he excelled in the refined art of grabbing, clutching, and clinging, which he used to blanket and antagonize opponents. In 1966, during a playoff series against Chicago, Watson held Bobby Hull to only one goal, earning the nickname "Super Pest." He later served a brief tenure as coach of the Edmonton Oilers.

 After 11 years with the Rangers and four with the Bruins, he came over to Detroit and skated with Howe, Delvecchio, and Bathgate. Who was he?

 Dean Prentice, who helped the Red Wings reach the 1966 Stanley Cup finals before falling to Montreal. With 860 points in 1,378 NHL games, Prentice is regarded by some hockey historians as among the best players not in the Hockey Hall of Fame.

 Andy Bathgate had won the Hart Trophy in 1959 with New York and a Stanley Cup with Toronto in 1964. How did he get to the Motor City?

 Chronic knee problems caused him to be shipped to the Red Wings. Bathgate, an athletic, graceful player who handled the puck with considerable flash, was one of the first to use the slapshot.

Bathgate is closely associated with what other hockey innovation?

 On November 1, 1959, while still with the Rangers, Bathgate sent one of his harder shots toward Montreal goalie Jacques Plante. The puck hit the All-Star goalie in the face, opening a bloody gash. When Plante returned to the ice, he was wearing a mask—a piece of equipment now used universally.

 Bathgate scored a total of six power-play goals in the '66 playoffs. With whom does he share that team record?

 Dino Ciccarelli, who had six in the 1995 and 1996 playoffs.

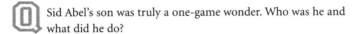

 Sid Abel's son was truly a one-game wonder. Who was he and what did he do?

Gerry Abel once said if he could be half as good as his father, he'd be happy. Such was not to be the case, however. Gerry's only NHL game came on March 8, 1967, a 3-1 defeat of the Rangers in New York. But at least the elder Abel, then coaching the team, got to see his boy skate with Gordie Howe.

Alex Delvecchio wore the "C" as team captain for 11 years—1963 to 1973. With whom did he share the role in 1974?

Six teammates: Nick Libett, Red Berenson, Gary Bergman, Ted Harris, Mickey Redmond, and Larry Johnston.

Name two team records held by Alex Delvecchio.

 Most consecutive games (548) and most winning goals by a rookie (6).

 He was with Detroit from 1961 to 1963 (leading the NHL in penalty minutes with 273) and back again in '67 and '68. Who was he?

 Howie Young, a native of Toronto. Young, an aspiring thespian, had a minor role in the 1965 film *None But The Brave*, starring Frank Sinatra.

 He was known as "the Red Baron" and had spent time with Montreal, New York, and St. Louis before joining a poor Detroit club in the early 1970s. Who was this center?

 Gordon Berenson, who scored 658 points in his 17-year NHL career. He later won two NCAA championships as coach at the University of Michigan.

The Red Wings celebrate after a victory in the 1961 Stanley Cup playoffs.
Coach Syd Abel is front and center, and captain Gordie Howe is to his right.

# CHAPTER FIVE
# LONG INTERREGNUM

The date was April 14, 1955, when the Wings took a 3-1 victory against Montreal at the Olympia, winning the Stanley Cup for the seventh time in franchise history. As coach Jimmy Skinner and his players—Sawchuk, Kelly, Goldham, Provonost, Woit, Hay, Hillman, Lindsay, Leswick, Howe, Delvecchio, Pavelich, Skov, Reibel, Wilson, Dineen, Stasiuk, and Bonin—circled the ice as champs, serenaded by their adoring fans, surely no one expected that 42 years would pass before the Wings would fly so high again.

Few top-quality prospects were coming up from the Detroit farm system, and questionable trades by Jack Adams robbed the team of many good and great players. The wave had crested, and things fell apart in 1959 when the Wings finished in last place, out of the playoffs for the first time in 20 years. Coach Sid Abel engineered a rejuvenation in the early and mid-1960s, but still brought home no Stanley Cups.

Then began what glib hockey historians like to call the "Dead Wings" era, when the team descended into mediocrity, making the NHL playoffs just twice from 1967 to 1983. The league had expanded from six to 12 teams in 1968, then to 14 in 1971, 16 in 1973, and 18 in 1975; some kind of expansion had, it must be admitted, been long overdue. At any rate, the Red Wings too often found themselves losing to such nouveau teams as the Los Angeles Kings, Pittsburgh Penguins, Oakland Seals, Philadelphia Flyers, St. Louis Blues, Minnesota North Stars, and Buffalo Sabres. To make matters even more galling, the home cities of such franchises often lacked the hockey culture that had taken root in Detroit over the decades.

Gordie Howe retired (from the Wings, at least) following the 1971 season, a fairly miserable one in which the team came in seventh in the NHL's East Division. There would be a new arena, new ownership, and a new generation of hockey fans before the Wings would once again be on top. Even the new accommodations did not help lure fans to see a talent-starved team, as the season ticket base slipped to about 2,000. It had been a slow, long decline for a proud organization, which by the early 1980s was saddled with debt and unable to field a contender.

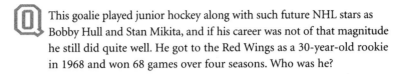 This goalie played junior hockey along with such future NHL stars as Bobby Hull and Stan Mikita, and if his career was not of that magnitude he still did quite well. He got to the Red Wings as a 30-year-old rookie in 1968 and won 68 games over four seasons. Who was he?

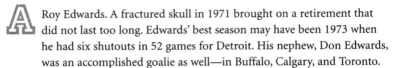 Roy Edwards. A fractured skull in 1971 brought on a retirement that did not last too long. Edwards' best season may have been 1973 when he had six shutouts in 52 games for Detroit. His nephew, Don Edwards, was an accomplished goalie as well—in Buffalo, Calgary, and Toronto.

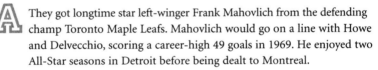 Who did the Red Wings acquire prior to the 1968 season?

They got longtime star left-winger Frank Mahovlich from the defending champ Toronto Maple Leafs. Mahovlich would go on a line with Howe and Delvecchio, scoring a career-high 49 goals in 1969. He enjoyed two All-Star seasons in Detroit before being dealt to Montreal.

What was Gordie Howe's last hat trick?

 He did it against Pittsburgh on November 2, 1969.

Who was "the Little Beaver"?

 Marcel Dionne, Detroit's top pick in the 1971 NHL draft. He spent four seasons with the Red Wings, 12 with the LA Kings, and his last four with the New York Rangers. Despite scoring 731 goals (fourth on the all-time list), Dionne never came close to being on a Stanley Cup winner.

 This man had played just 11 games for the Bruins over two seasons (1969 and 1970) and did not score a single goal. By '71, however, he was with the Wings and his career came to life; he scored 67 points for Doug Barkley's team. Who was he?

 Tom Webster. The next year, he was one of many NHL players who opted to jump to the new World Hockey Association. Webster, who retired in 1980, later coached for the Los Angeles Kings.

 Nevin D. "Ned" Harkness was hired as Detroit's new coach in 1971. What was his NHL background?

 He had none. Harkness never played or coached in the league. A native of Ottawa, Ontario, he had enjoyed considerable success coaching lacrosse and hockey at Rensselaer Polytechnic and Cornell (where one of his goalies was Ken Dryden). Harkness' teams won two NCAA titles, so perhaps that is why the Red Wings management decided to give him a try.

How did Harkness do behind the bench?

 Not too well. His team went 12-22-4 before he was replaced by Doug Barkley. However, Harkness was promoted to general manager and remained in that position for three seasons as the Wings never got higher than fifth place. Harkness was unable to duplicate his collegiate success in the National Hockey League. He had trouble guiding and motivating veteran players, and there were other problems within the organization that can't be blamed on him. Nevertheless, this era is recalled rather unkindly as "Darkness with Harkness," one of the worst in franchise history.

 On January 2, 1971, the Wings met the Maple Leafs in Toronto. Who prevailed in that contest?

 Toronto, 13-0. It remains one of the worst losses in Red Wings history.

 This player was mired in the minor leagues until the NHL decided to double in size from six teams to 12 in 1968. He proved his abilities with the North Stars, Canadiens, Red Wings, Rangers, Flyers, and Caps, but his best years were in Detroit. Name him if you can.

 Right-winger Bill Collins, who rang up 82 points for Johnny Wilson's team in 1972 and 1973.

He played nearby at the University of Michigan, spent five seasons (1971–1975) with some mediocre Red Wings teams, and later coached the Blues and Sabres. Who was he?

Gordon "Red" Berenson, who returned to his alma mater and coached the Wolverines for 17 seasons. He had been with Montreal when the Habs won the '65 Stanley Cup and appeared on the April 9, 1968, cover of *Sports Illustrated* while playing with the Blues.

This right-winger had won a couple of Stanley Cups with Montreal before coming to Detroit in 1971 in the Frank Mahovlich trade. Who was he?

Mickey Redmond, who had a slapshot some likened to a howitzer. He scored 103 goals in his first two seasons with the Wings. Soon, however, he was suffering back problems that eventually drove him from the ice. In 1976, Redmond retired prematurely at age 29, but he later served as a team broadcaster. His brother Dick was a defenseman—primarily with the Chicago Black Hawks and the Boston Bruins—for 13 seasons.

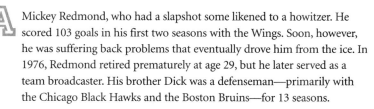

This native of Verdun, Quebec, played for Detroit in the early 1970s and later served as interim coach of the Flames and Mighty Ducks. Name him. Hint: Despite an 11-year career that encompassed 734 games, he never reached the Stanley Cup playoffs—an NHL record.

Guy Charron.

How did Detroit's four major league pro sports teams do in 1975?

 The Lions won 7 and lost 7, the Pistons were 40-42 (losing in the first round of the NBA playoffs), the Tigers were 57-102, and the Red Wings were right with them: 23-45-12. Not a good year for sports in the Motor City.

 The Red Wings caused a stir when they signed a talented blueliner from Sweden at the end of the 1972 season. Other NHL teams were soon looking for such players, rather than just those in the far-flung Canadian provinces. Who was he?

 Thommie Bergman, who scored 21 points for Detroit in 1973. Targeted by thugs on other teams, he soon jumped to the Winnipeg Jets of the WHA. Bergman was back with the Wings in 1978, the first time they reached the playoffs in eight years. To be fair, however, we must give credit to one Ulf Sterner, a Swede who signed with the New York Rangers back in 1964. He was so abused by opponents and teammates that he gave up after four games and returned to Scandinavia. In the 40-plus years since Sterner's inauspicious debut, Swedes have become some of the most respected citizens in the league of nations that is the NHL.

 Brian Conacher, a center on the 1972 Detroit team, was the son of what famous person?

 Lionel Conacher, who played for the Montreal Maroons and Chicago Black Hawks, was voted Canada's top male athlete of the half-century in 1950 and spent many years in Parliament. Other members of that family included the Red Wings' Charlie Conacher and Roy Conacher.

In 1974, Gordie Howe came out of retirement to join his sons on the forward line with the Houston Aeros of the World Hockey Association. Which of the two younger Howes later came to play for the Wings?

 Mark Howe. He had spent 10 seasons with the Philadelphia Flyers, but his numbers were already in steep decline when he got to Detroit in 1993. The fact that he scored just eight goals in three seasons indicates that Howe was more of a novelty than anything else. Still, he had a very solid career—six seasons in the WHA and 16 in the NHL. Despite the huge shadow cast by his father, Mark Howe was one of the best two-way defensemen of the 1980s, three times was a runner-up for the Norris Trophy, and thrice reached the Stanley Cup finals. He retired in 1995 and became a scout and administrator in the Red Wings organization.

 Henry Boucha was a full-blooded Ojibwa Indian, attended the University of Detroit, and wore a trademark red headband in the days before mandatory helmets. He was a good pivot man for the Red Wings in the early 1970s, but he is best remembered for what incident?

 On January 4, 1975, while playing with the Minnesota North Stars, Boucha was involved in an ugly stick-swinging incident with Dave Forbes of the Bruins. It left him with a cracked bone around his eye and blurred vision. Criminal charges were filed against Forbes, but the case ended with a hung jury. Boucha was never the same after the traumatic injury.

Walt McKechnie was truly a hockey nomad. Where did he play?

 A rookie center with the Minnesota North Stars in 1969, he changed major league teams 12 times and was in the minors on four occasions. In fact, he was once on the rosters of four different clubs over a 12-month period. All told, at the NHL level, McKechnie skated for the North Stars, Golden Seals, Bruins, Wings (1975–1977 and 1982–1983), Capitals, Barons, Leafs, and Rockies. Only three times did his teams get to the playoffs.

 The last four or five years of Gordie Howe's career in Detroit had been a harbinger of things to come as the team slid into a long funk that did not end until the late 1980s. What were the worst of those teams?

 The 1977 team was 16-55-9, the 1981 team was 19-43-18, and the 1986 team was 17-57-6.

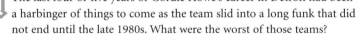 He was a product of Minnesota youth hockey, and three seasons under coach Herb Brooks at the University of Minnesota molded him into a fine defenseman. With the Red Wings, he was runner-up for the Calder Trophy in 1978 and spent a decade in Detroit. Name him.

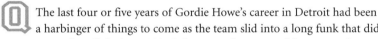 Reed Larson, who would have five 20-goal seasons. Team captain from 1980 to 1982, he was the sixth defenseman (and the first American) to score 200 career goals. Larson finished his NHL days with the Oilers, Islanders, North Stars, and Sabres.

What rugged defenseman, who played 11 games for the Red Wings in 1979 and 22 for the North Stars in 1980, became a minor cult hero by playing himself in the classic hockey movie *Slapshot?*

Dave Hanson.

 Except for one brief detour to the minors, this defenseman was with the Wings from 1974 through 1981. He then moved on to the Nordiques and then the Canadiens. Who was he?

Jean Hamel. His career came to a premature end while in Montreal when he was hit in the eye with a puck. Hamel's vision was impaired, and he was through.

He was a mainstay on Detroit's blueline for six years (scoring 89 points) before being traded to Washington in 1987. Who was he?

John Barrett, whose career was cut short by a broken kneecap.

Four players hold the team record for most short-handed playoff goals (four) in a career. Name them.

 Gordie Howe, Sergei Fedorov, Kris Draper, and Kirk Maltby.

 Left-winger Nick Libett (a Wing from 1968 to 1979) was an asset at both ends of the ice. He recorded six 20-goal seasons and peaked in 1972 with 31 while playing on a line with Marcel Dionne and Bill Collins. How many times did Detroit reach the playoffs during Libett's 11 years there?

 Just twice—1970 and 1978.

 He scored 16 goals as a rookie pivot with the 1975 Red Wings playing on a line with Nick Libett and Bill Hogaboam. He was a solid role player for four and a half years in Motown and helped the team reach the playoffs in '78 for the first time in eight seasons. Name this native of Forest, Ontario.

Bill Lochead. After getting put on waivers by Detroit, he played briefly with the Rockies and Rangers before spending two full decades with a variety of European clubs.

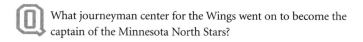 What journeyman center for the Wings went on to become the captain of the Minnesota North Stars?

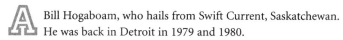 Bill Hogaboam, who hails from Swift Current, Saskatchewan. He was back in Detroit in 1979 and 1980.

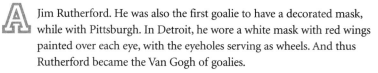 Name the diminutive goaltender who, in February 1976, tied a team record held by Dolly Dolson, Glenn Hall, and Terry Sawchuk with three straight shutouts—against Washington, Toronto, and Minnesota.

Jim Rutherford. He was also the first goalie to have a decorated mask, while with Pittsburgh. In Detroit, he wore a white mask with red wings painted over each eye, with the eyeholes serving as wheels. And thus Rutherford became the Van Gogh of goalies.

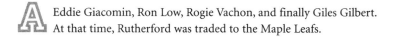 Who were some of the men Rutherford had to battle to keep his job in Detroit?

Eddie Giacomin, Ron Low, Rogie Vachon, and finally Giles Gilbert. At that time, Rutherford was traded to the Maple Leafs.

He was in the Canadiens' minor league system before joining the Red Wings on October 10, 1977, and stayed there for seven seasons, never playing fewer than 57 games. Who was he?

 Paul Woods, whose first year in Detroit was his best—19 goals and 23 assists for 42 points.

 Vaclav Nedomansky, a Wing for five years, was at his best in 1980 when he had 74 points. What was so special about him?

 A big hockey star in Czechoslovakia, he had been an indispensable player on two medal-winning Olympic teams. In 1974, while the Iron Curtain was very much a reality, Nedomansky defected to Toronto via Switzerland and played for a couple of WHA clubs before signing with Detroit. He was not able to return to his home country until many years later.

 This player, who grew up in a small town in Saskatchewan, joined the Red Wings in 1975 and gave them some toughness at a time when they needed it. He is best known for irritating the Colorado Rockies' Wilf Paiement so much that the latter whacked him with his stick, provoking a lawsuit that brought an $850,000 settlement. Name him.

Dennis Polonich. Although he stood just 5' 6", he was known to throw leather at everything that moved—even his own teammates. Polonich was the Wings' fevered little madman who would fight anyone, size be damned. Three years after the Paiement matter, he was sent to the minors where he finished up.

The 1977 Wings were pretty bad, winning just 16 games. When was the last time a Detroit team won so few?

 The 1938 team won only 12 games, but they also played far fewer— 48, as opposed to 80.

 A fixture with the Black Hawks for more than a decade, the brother of "the Golden Jet," and the uncle of a future Red Wing, he came to Detroit for one last season in 1978. To whom do we refer?

 Dennis Hull. His brother was Bobby, and his nephew was Brett.

 In 1958, this goalie had attended a Red Wings training camp but evidently did not impress. Things turned out well for him, however, as he became one of the most successful and popular players ever to wear the uniform of the New York Rangers. He took part in more than 500 regular-season games with the Blueshirts and helped the team reach the Stanley Cup playoffs nine straight years. After being put on waivers, he landed back in Detroit. Who was he?

 Ed Giacomin. When the Red Wings met the Rangers at Madison Square Garden a few days later, the fans serenaded him almost the whole game. Giacomin retired early in the 1978 season with a résumé that listed 54 shutouts and nearly 300 wins.

After an excellent amateur career, center Dale McCourt was expected to be an NHL superstar but he never quite got to that level—although he scored 33 goals during his rookie year (1978) in Detroit. What legal matter derailed him soon thereafter?

 McCourt was awarded to Los Angeles as compensation after Detroit signed LA Kings goalie Rogie Vachon, but he refused to report. A nasty court battle was resolved and McCourt stayed with the Wings, but his play seemed to stagnate. The enigmatic center later played with Buffalo, Toronto, and a team in Switzerland.

 Bobby Kromm was in his first year as the team's coach in 1978. How did he do?

 Under Kromm, a native of Calgary, Alberta, the Wings had their best finish since 1965. They were second in the standings that year behind the Montreal Canadiens, eventually losing to them in the second round of the playoffs.

 Name the defenseman who was with Detroit from 1979 to 1983 and hastened his departure when he got into a dispute with Jim Devellano, calling the Wings' GM a liar.

 Willie Huber, who was shipped forthwith to New York. At 6' 5" and 228 pounds, Huber was the biggest player in the NHL, something of a Gulliver among Lilliputians. Because of his size, some fans expected him to be a nasty physical presence, which was not his nature.

How did the Red Wings come to leave Olympia Stadium?

 In the late 1970s, some developers from suburban Pontiac sought to get the team to move to a proposed arena next to the Silverdome (then home of the Lions). A package worth $3 million in annual profits looked good, but Detroit Mayor Coleman Young was determined not to let that happen. The city built Joe Louis Arena for $53 million—much of it federal money—downtown, next to Cobo Hall along with a couple of parking structures, then offered it all to the Wings at a huge discount.

 What was the last game played at the Olympia?

 On December 15, 1979, the Red Wings met the Quebec Nordiques before 15,609 patrons. It ended up in a 4-4 tie.

 Who scored the last goal in that game at Olympia Stadium?

 The Red Wings' Greg Joly, with an assist from Paul Woods.

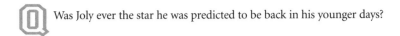

 Was Joly ever the star he was predicted to be back in his younger days?

No, but it was not entirely his own fault. Joly, a native of Calgary, Alberta, was chosen first overall by the expansion Washington Capitols in 1974 and was rushed into the NHL before he was ready. He was traded to Detroit and spent the better part of six years there. A solid blueliner who started moving down the depth charts, Joly's career lasted 365 games.

 How many people does Joe Louis Arena hold for hockey?

19,983.

What was the first hockey game at Joe Louis Arena?

The Red Wings lost to St. Louis, 3-2, on December 27, 1979, with 19,742 fans looking on. Brian Sutter of the Blues scored the first goal ever at the new rink.

What became of the Olympia?

 It was razed in 1986. A U.S. National Guard armory stands there now, and a plaque commemorates Olympia Stadium and what it meant to Detroit for a half-century. Truthfully, its last 20 years had not been good. Shortly after team owner Bruce Norris spent $25 million to expand and upgrade the facility, the July 1967 riot took place, killing 43 people. The surrounding neighborhood grew shabby and dangerous, the depletion of the city's population accelerated, and a crumbling urban landscape was left behind. The once-glorious Olympia was a sad example of that decay—graffiti everywhere, a leaking roof, broken railings, littered aisles, and parking lots surrounded by barbed wire.

 At home, the 1981 Red Wings won 16 games, lost 15, and tied 9. How were they on the road?

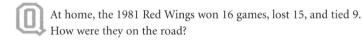 Downright abysmal, posting a record of 3-28-9.

 Defenseman Greg Smith was traded by the Minnesota North Stars to Detroit in 1981 and was a Red Wing for five seasons before moving on to Washington. Where did he play collegiately?

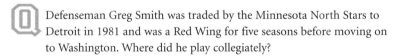 Colorado College.

In what field did owner Mike Ilitch make his fortune?

 Pizza. A second-generation Macedonian-American, this Detroit native founded Little Caesars Pizza in 1959, which he successfully franchised. Ilitch, who is now worth an estimated $1.5 billion, bought the Red Wings from Bruce Norris in 1982 for $11 million and saw its value grow many times over. Ten years later, Ilitch purchased the Detroit Tigers for $85 million from Tom Monaghan, who was himself a pizza magnate (Domino's). Ilitch, who has no shortage of critics—especially regarding his ownership of the Tigers and his downtown real estate maneuvers—nevertheless has quite a life history. His advice: "Be humble and never toot your own horn. If you do something good, people will find out."

 What were some of Ilitch's moves after buying the Wings?

 He invested money in the recruitment of players from all over the world and upgraded Joe Louis Arena. Attendance soon reached record levels (season ticket sales surpassed 16,000), aided in part by Ilitch's marketing efforts, which included giving away new cars during games. After the team reached the Stanley Cup semis in 1987 and 1988, Detroit was among the NHL's most valuable franchises and Ilitch was one of the best owners, known for treating his players like family and sometimes handing out spontaneous bonuses for good play.

What man is now in his 25th year with the Red Wings and his 40th in the NHL?

 Jim Devellano, a Toronto native who never played pro hockey but knows the game inside and out. He began as a scout with the St. Louis Blues in 1967 when the NHL expanded from six to 12 teams. When the New York Islanders were founded in 1972, he scouted there as they went on to win four straight Stanley Cups (1980–1983). By 1982, he had been hired by Red Wings owner Mike Ilitch, serving as GM and senior vice president. Devellano was at the helm as the Red Wings steadily rose from one of the NHL's weak sisters into the powerful club that lifted the coveted Cup in triumph three times.

 Name a few of Devellano's actions as the Red Wings' GM.

 In 1983, in his first draft he tabbed future Hall-of-Famer Steve Yzerman; he was one of the first NHL general managers to assemble a strong European scouting staff, which led to such standouts as Sergei Fedorov, Slava Kozlov, Vladimir Konstantinov, Nicklas Lidstrom, and Tomas Holmstrom; he tutored three current GMs—Ken Holland of Detroit, Darcy Reiger of the Buffalo Sabres, and Don Waddell of the Atlanta Thrashers; and he urged the hiring of coach Scotty Bowman in 1994. Since 2001, Devellano has been a top executive with the Detroit Tigers, another Ilitch property.

Was Yzerman a sure-fire prospect when he was drafted?

 Not really. The Wings were hoping to pick Olympic hero Pat LaFontaine, but the Rangers got him first so they "settled" for the small (5' 11" and 160 pounds) right-winger who had grown up in the suburbs of Ottawa. With a stellar rookie season, Yzerman proved to be a fine player who only got better with time. He became captain at age 21 and kept that honor until his retirement. A man who lifted the team when it was down—Detroit's last winning season before he arrived was 1973—Yzerman became a beloved figure; in an age of free agents and mercenaries, he stayed in the Motor City for 22 seasons. He won a lot of awards, helped the Wings win three Cups, and played for Canada's gold-medal winner in the Salt Lake City Olympics.

 He was a real sniper for the Buffalo Sabres, twice scoring more than 50 goals in a season. Although he no longer put up such numbers by the time the Red Wings had him (1982–1986), he played well. Who was this native of Nelson, British Columbia?

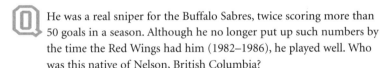 Danny Gare. He was a respected player, having been chosen captain in both Buffalo and Detroit.

 Name the rookie who led the Wings in scoring (26 goals and 41 assists) in 1982.

 Mark Osborne. He played one more season in Detroit before moving on to New York, Toronto, and Winnipeg, but he never exceeded those numbers.

This young man played every game of the 1982 and 1983 seasons with the Wings, scoring 96 points, but the coaches could not convince him to play defense. So he was soon shipped to the Rangers. Name him.

 Right-winger Mike Blaisdell.

 This center, a native of Peace River, Alberta, had enough speed, hockey sense, and character to make it for a dozen years in the NHL— beginning with Detroit from 1983 to 1986. During that time, he had three 60-point seasons. Identify him.

 Kelly Kisio, who was later sent to the New York Rangers in return for goalie Glen Hanlon. It was more of the same on Broadway, as he averaged nearly 70 points in five seasons and served as the team's captain much of that time.

 Who, besides Steve Yzerman, was chosen by Detroit in the 1983 NHL entry draft?

Bob "the Bad One" Probert, who is regarded by hockey aficionados as one of the greatest fighters the game has ever known. In one season alone, he had nearly 400 penalty minutes. Probert's problems with cocaine, alcohol, and law enforcement are part of his legacy. He spent nine months in a federal prison and was banned by the NHL, although that didn't last too long. A talented player but a goon nonetheless, Probert brawled with such men as Craig Coxe, Tie Domi, Marty McSorley, Todd Ewen, Troy Crowder, Tony Twist, Donald Brashear, Stu Grimson, Bob McGill, Dave Semenko, and Jay Caufield.

How did Probert's rambunctious tenure with the Red Wings end?

In the summer of 1994, Probert crashed his motorcycle into a car while riding in a Detroit suburb. His blood-alcohol level was thrice the legal limit. Five days later, the Red Wings announced that Probert was no longer part of the team. "This is the end," said club GM Jim Devellano. "[In] my 12 years with the organization...we've never spent more time on one player and his problems than we have on Probert." He spent his last five relatively unproductive years with the Blackhawks (Chicago's new name as of the mid-1980s) before retiring.

A scoring sensation in junior hockey in Ontario, this man became a solid two-way center for the Bruins, Rockies, Devils, and Red Wings. In 1984, his strong play helped Detroit reach the playoffs for the first time in six years. Name him.

Dwight Foster.

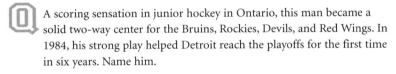

Identify the Red Wings' first black player.

The year was 1984, and the man was Brian Johnson, a right-winger from Montreal. He was up from the minors briefly—three games is very brief—and went scoreless before being sent back down. Johnson, the eighth black player in NHL history, retired in 1986.

What undersized goalie played one game for Hartford in 1981 and three for Detroit in 1984?

 Ken Holland, the Red Wings' GM since 1998. It's safe to say his exploits in management far have exceeded those as a player. Holland knew he wanted to stay in the game, so he served as the western scout before taking other positions within the organization, eventually being named general manager. A fairly aggressive wheeler and dealer, he won a Stanley Cup in his first year as GM. His admirers say Holland merits more credit for making the Red Wings perennial Stanley Cup contenders. He has deftly handled veterans' contracts and signed newcomers, too.

 Colin Campbell dressed for five teams (including the Wings from 1983 to 1985) in his decade-long NHL career. He accumulated more than 100 penalty minutes in most of those seasons and was known for fighting, hitting, checking, and harassing opponents to no end. So it is somewhat ironic that he later came to hold what position in the league's hierarchy?

 As executive vice-president and director of hockey operations, Campbell is called upon to adjudicate the nefarious on-ice actions of NHL players. Under his reign, Campbell has handed down some rather lengthy suspensions. He had paid his dues along the way, serving five years as an assistant coach in Detroit and four running the show in New York. During the 2005 NHL lockout, Campbell chaired a committee that studied ways to adjust NHL rules, resulting in major changes implemented the next season.

This native of Zrenjanin, Yugoslavia, had a 15-year NHL career with six clubs (Boston, California, Chicago, Atlanta, Vancouver, and Detroit) from 1971 to 1985. He was an elegant center, one of hockey's best stick handlers. Can you identify him?

 Ivan Boldirev. Halfway through the 1983 season, he was traded to the Detroit Red Wings for journeyman forward Mark Kirton. With a late-career resurgence, Boldirev scored 35 goals in 1984, helping the Wings reach the playoffs for only the second time in twelve years. He and rookie Steve Yzerman combined to form a fine one-two punch down the middle. He hit the 1,000-game mark in 1985 before retiring.

 Greg Stefan, a Detroit goalie from 1983 to 1990, grew up in Brantford, Ontario. Who was one of his teammates as a schoolboy?

 Wayne Gretzky. Stefan's Wings made a run for the Cup in '87 and '88, losing both times to Edmonton, led by the Great One. Stefan liked to control the ice around his net. An altercation with Al Secord of the Blackhawks cost him an eight-game suspension, and another with Pittsburgh forward Dan Frawley set Stefan down for six more games.

 This offensively gifted left-winger was with the Wings for most of eight seasons, peaking in 1985 when he scored 55 goals and finished fourth behind Wayne Gretzky, Jari Kurri, and Mike Bossy. He was a first-team All-Star that year. Who was he?

 John Ogrodnick. During his 14-year career, he also spent time with the Quebec Nordiques and New York Rangers.

The Presidents' Trophy, for most team points, was first awarded in 1986. When has Detroit won it?

 In 1995, 1996, 2002, 2004, and 2006.

 This blueliner came out of New England, started with the Blackhawks, and then had five solid years in Boston before donning red and white in 1987. Name him if you can.

 Mike O'Connell. Coach Jacques Demers used him as a penalty killer and defensive stabilizer on his squad. O'Connell adapted well and helped the Wings reach the semis in 1987 and 1988. After playing in his 13th season in 1990, he hung up his skates. He did, however, serve six years as GM of the Bruins.

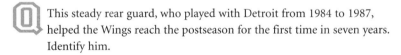

 This steady rear guard, who played with Detroit from 1984 to 1987, helped the Wings reach the postseason for the first time in seven years. Identify him.

 Randy Ladouceur, who later played for Hartford and Anaheim. A respected presence on and off the ice wherever he played, Ladouceur is now an assistant coach for the Maple Leafs.

 What team record was set on November 25, 1987, in a game against Winnipeg?

Gerard Gallant, Adam Oates, Mel Bridgman, Jeff Sharples, and Brent Ashton scored goals 4:54 apart.

111

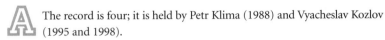

Two players share the Detroit record for most game-winning goals in one playoff season. Who were they?

The record is four; it is held by Petr Klima (1988) and Vyacheslav Kozlov (1995 and 1998).

In 1985, Detroit owner Mike Ilitch and GM Jim Devellano gave this player from NCAA champion Rensselaer Polytechnic Institute a deal worth $1 million over four years—at that time the richest rookie contract ever. That fact did not exactly endear him to teammates and opponents, and he was traded to the St. Louis Blues after four years. Who was he, and was it a wise trade?

Adam Oates is the person in question, and the trade was awful from a Red Wings perspective. The guys Detroit got were of minimal value, whereas Oates, a hard-working forward, became one of the NHL's top passing centers and setup men. He was a five-time All-Star with the Blues, Bruins, Capitols, Flyers, Mighty Ducks, and Oilers, and led two of those teams to the Stanley Cup finals. Oates retired with the sixth-most assists in league history.

Detroit has had many minor league hockey teams over the years. Name a few of them.

The Detroit Junior Red Wings, the Detroit Hettche, the Motor City Mechanics, the Detroit Olympics, the Detroit Adrays, the Detroit Greyhounds, the Detroit Junior Whalers, the Detroit Little Caesars, the Detroit Mundus, the Detroit Holzbaugh, the Detroit Mansfields, the Detroit Millionaires, the Detroit Nationals, the Detroit Pontiacs, and the Detroit Vipers, among others.

Who was the overall No. 1 pick in the 1986 draft?

 Joe Murphy, chosen by Detroit. A right-winger, he helped Michigan State win the NCAA hockey championship before going pro. Murphy spent just over three seasons as a Red Wing before being traded to Edmonton, just in time to win the 1990 Cup with the Oilers. In a 15-year career that also included stops in Chicago, St. Louis, San Jose, Boston, and Washington, Murphy played in 779 regular-season games, compiling 233 goals and 295 assists.

 This man with the long hair and good looks, who came out of northern Ontario along with Dale McCourt, was with the New York Rangers when they advanced to the Stanley Cup finals in 1979. He was traded to Detroit and had a pair of productive 80-game seasons, but another trade (to Pittsburgh) seemed to take the steam out of his career. He played for two other teams, languished in the minors for a while, and then quit at age 41. Identify him.

 Ron Duguay, who played right wing and center.

 A sixth-round pick in 1981, this left-winger showed a tenacity that impressed the Detroit brass. He was ready for the rough and tumble of the NHL, and won a spot with the Wings by 1985. Who was he?

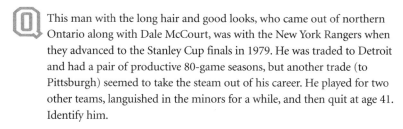 Gerard "Turk" Gallant. Tough though he may have been, he suffered a broken jaw in a fight with Dirk Graham of the North Stars. His most productive offensive season came in 1989 when he had 39 goals, but 230 penalty minutes. Coach Jacques Demers said that perhaps Gallant's bully-boy ways were holding him back from a 50-goal season.

What did Gallant do after his playing days were done?

 He served as coach of the Columbus Blue Jackets for three seasons.

 Petr Klima was a talented but hard-drinking forward who could play both wings, a fast skater with excellent puck-handling skills. How did he come to be a member of the Detroit club?

 According to rampant rumor, the Wings tried to bribe Czechoslovakian authorities to get Klima out of his native country. True or not, in the summer of 1985 he became the first Czech player to defect to an American-based team rather than one of the league's Canadian teams, which had done such smuggling for years. U.S. Attorney General Edwin Meese helped expedite the political asylum process for Klima, who spoke no English upon arrival. Fortunately, the Wings brought his girlfriend to the States as well. He scored 32 goals as a rookie and kept up that pace for four seasons with the Red Wings, but most observers agreed he could have done much more. He was traded to Edmonton in 1990 and helped the Oilers win the Cup that year.

 How did Klima do in the 1988 Stanley Cup playoffs?

 It was the high point of his tenure with the Wings, as he scored 10 goals to break a mark set by Gordie Howe in 1955. Klima had the advantage of playing in four more games, however.

What number did Klima wear throughout his NHL career?

 85, in honor of the year the Red Wings brought him to the West.

 A hot-tempered star with the Leafs for more than a decade and then a couple of years with the Flyers, he came to Detroit in 1985 for one last season—and a desultory one it was. Name him.

 Darryl Sittler. He struggled to get ice time under coach Nick Polano and ended up with the worst goals-per-game average of his career. The Red Wings bought out Sittler's contract when the season was over.

 Brad Park won a lot of fame during his time with the Rangers and Bruins. What is his connection with the Red Wings?

 Park, who once drew comparisons with Bobby Orr for his offensive skill, stickhandling, and pugnacity in New York and Boston, signed a free-agent contract with the Red Wings in 1984. Still an effective player but hobbled by knee injuries, he announced his retirement after two years in Detroit.

 Park also served briefly as Detroit's coach. How did that go?

 Quite badly. He replaced Harry Neale after 35 games in the 1986 season and proceeded to compile a record of 9-34-2. Thus ended Park's coaching career, as Jacques Demers was hired.

This native of Summerside, Prince Edward Island, got his first taste of NHL action in 1984 with the Canadiens, scoring 43 points. He had three years with the Penguins and three with the Red Wings, but his career was at a standstill, so he journeyed to Europe. Who was he?

John Chabot, who made a nice living as a player for several teams in Italy, Switzerland, and Germany.

From 1980 to 1986, this man with the mullet haircut played for the Jets, Maple Leafs, and Red Wings. A defenseman, he scored just 33 points while compiling 728 penalty minutes. Who was he?

Barry Melrose, a native of Kelvington, Saskatchewan. He became coach of the LA Kings, who reached the Stanley Cup finals in 1993. His star player, Wayne Gretzky, called Melrose "the greatest coach I ever played for," but soon soured on him and pulled strings to get him fired. Melrose would go on to become a TV hockey commentator.

There was a man on the 1985 Detroit team with a well-noted penchant for pugilism. Who was he? Hint: His name was not Bob Probert (Probert would arrive the next year). One more hint: He had played six years with the Maple Leafs and five with the Canucks.

Dave "Tiger" Williams, the league's all-time leader in penalty minutes. Always willing to skirmish with opposing tough guys, he insisted that he did not deserve so much time in the sin bin, but some people said he should have been given even more. With the Red Wings that year, he had 11 points and 158 penalty minutes in 55 games.

Who is the only man to have won the Jack Adams Award for coach of the year in consecutive seasons?

 Jacques Demers of the Red Wings, who won it in 1987 and 1988.

 What other Detroit coaches have won it?

 Just two—Bobby Kromm in 1978 and Scotty Bowman in 1996.

 Demers was with Detroit from 1987 to 1990, and later won a Stanley Cup as coach of the Canadiens. What startling fact did he reveal in his 1993 autobiography?

 That in spite of all his success, Demers was illiterate.

 Who led the NHL in shutouts in the 1988 season?

 The Wings' Glen Hanlon, who had four. Some people had considered him the best goalie in the game when he was younger, but a series of injuries tended to put him out of action rather often. As well respected in Detroit as he had been in Vancouver and New York, he retired in 1991.

 Who was Bruce Martyn?

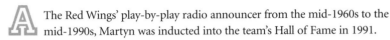 The Red Wings' play-by-play radio announcer from the mid-1960s to the mid-1990s, Martyn was inducted into the team's Hall of Fame in 1991.

This Swede was with Toronto from 1974 to 1989 and was one of the best defensemen of his era. He joined the Red Wings for one final NHL season in 1990. Who was he?

 Borje Salming.

Steve Yzerman had quite an offensive season in 1989. What team records did he set?

 Most goals (65), most assists (90), and, of course, most points (155). He was joined that year on the line by Gerard Gallant and Paul MacLean.

He was captain of the Calgary Flames when they won the Stanley Cup in 1989 and was a fine blueliner for the Wings for three seasons. Who was he?

 Brad McCrimmon. He then moved on to the Whalers and Coyotes before retiring.

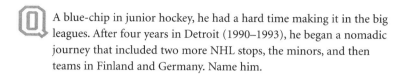 A blue-chip in junior hockey, he had a hard time making it in the big leagues. After four years in Detroit (1990–1993), he began a nomadic journey that included two more NHL stops, the minors, and then teams in Finland and Germany. Name him.

 Yves Racine, a utility defender wherever he went.

 Shawn Burr spent parts of 16 seasons in the NHL, primarily with the Red Wings. A hard-nosed worker in the trenches who could also put the puck in the net, he scored a career high of 24 goals in what year?

 1990.

 What team records did Burr set in 1987?

 In the Stanley Cup playoffs, he had seven goals and nine points— the most ever for a rookie.

 What Red Wings center (1990–1993) had grown up in the leafy Detroit suburb of Grosse Point? Hint: He didn't like playing second fiddle to Steve Yzerman and forced a trade back to Los Angeles, from whence he had come.

Jimmy Carson, who is actually of Greek origin; his grandfather changed the ancestral name from Kyriazopoulos to Carson.

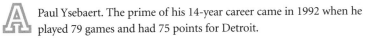 He had played collegiately at Bowling Green, was with the Wings in the early 1990s, and later became captain of the Tampa Bay Lightning. Who was he?

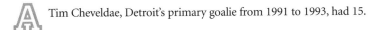 Paul Ysebaert. The prime of his 14-year career came in 1992 when he played 79 games and had 75 points for Detroit.

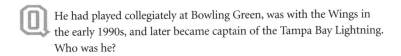 Who holds the team record for most assists by a goaltender?

Tim Cheveldae, Detroit's primary goalie from 1991 to 1993, had 15.

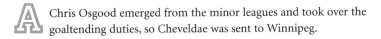 Cheveldae was a workhorse for the Wings, especially in 1992 when he took part in 72 games and was chosen for the All-Star Game. What led to his departure from the Motor City?

Chris Osgood emerged from the minor leagues and took over the goaltending duties, so Cheveldae was sent to Winnipeg.

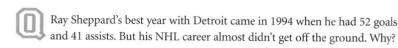

Ray Sheppard's best year with Detroit came in 1994 when he had 52 goals and 41 assists. But his NHL career almost didn't get off the ground. Why?

After Sheppard (a right-winger) was drafted by the Sabres in 1984, he and his agent chose not to sign a contract so that Sheppard could stay in the minor leagues and improve his skills, and—theoretically—the money he would be paid in the NHL. The gamble appeared to have been foolish when his numbers initially dropped off; they picked up, however, and he was on the all-rookie team with Buffalo in 1988. He played for 14 seasons, so perhaps Sheppard and his agent made the right call back in '84.

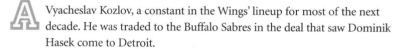

This pivot man, who came from Voskresensk, USSR, was fast and a capable scorer. His first full year with Detroit was in 1994, when he scored 34 goals in 77 games. Name him.

Vyacheslav Kozlov, a constant in the Wings' lineup for most of the next decade. He was traded to the Buffalo Sabres in the deal that saw Dominik Hasek come to Detroit.

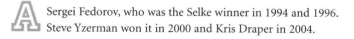

The Selke Trophy for best defensive forward was first awarded in 1978, but the Wings did not have a winner until 1994. Who was he?

Sergei Fedorov, who was the Selke winner in 1994 and 1996. Steve Yzerman won it in 2000 and Kris Draper in 2004.

Jim Rutherford, the diminutive goalie who recorded three straight shutouts in February 1976. Note the face mask with Red Wings logos—an NHL first.

# CHAPTER SIX
# RAISING THE
# CUP ONCE AGAIN

Perhaps it's a stretch to compare Mike Ilitch's impact on the Red Wings with that of James Norris, Sr., but we can safely say the franchise owes both men thanks many times over. Ilitch, Detroit-born and -raised, must have known what he was getting into by making that $11 million purchase in 1982 from the Norris estate. He found a dysfunctional organization that was living on past glory and unable to regain its place among the elite of the NHL. Ilitch and his new GM, Jim Devellano, set out to change that.

Attendance improved along with the quality of play—helped in large part by Steve Yzerman and other talented young players. The Red Wings were in the title chase once again, losing in the Stanley Cup semifinals in 1987 and 1988. It would not really come together until 1994 when Ilitch hired the NHL's most successful coach, Scotty Bowman, to mold that talent and bring in some complementary veterans to forge a champion. They made it through three rounds before losing to New Jersey in the 1995 finals and came close again in 1996.

Detroit had served notice that it was once again a serious contender. The Wings swept Philly in the 1997 Stanley Cup finals and did the same the next year to Washington (with a wheelchair-bound Vladimir Konstantinov looking on), culminating quite a turnaround for what had until recently been a sad-sack franchise. Retooling its roster after the turn of the century, Detroit got some vets (including Chris Chelios, Pat Verbeek, Luc Robitaille, Brett Hull, and Dominik Hasek) who fit well with Bowman's system. In 2002, the Red Wings had a league-best regular-season 116 points and claimed a 10th Stanley Cup by beating the Carolina Hurricanes in four. As if Bowman's legacy needed any more validation, that was his ninth championship. With health issues nagging at him, he stepped down as coach but remained a consultant with the team.

Soon the NHL's focus was not so much on the ice but in the board rooms, where league and team management negotiated with players' representatives over a new collective bargaining agreement. The small-market clubs were losing money hand over fist and claimed they could not compete fairly against the big boys. They would not be satisfied with anything short of a salary cap, more in line with the kind of revenues the NHL could generate. The players were having none of it, insisting the owners had only themselves to blame for foolish spending. This, in a nutshell, is why the NHL cancelled its 2005 season.

After much posturing and finger-pointing (and perhaps realizing the damage being done to the sport), the two sides finally hammered out a deal that included a salary cap and rule changes to enhance the flow of the game. Two years after so much drama, it remains to be seen whether competitive balance and fiscal responsibility are possible in the National Hockey League. In all likelihood, strong franchises like Detroit—now valued at $240 million—will continue to find a way to succeed.

 What was the most convincing home opener in team history?

 In 1995, the Wings beat Edmonton, 9-0, at Joe Louis Arena. A 7-0 defeat of Boston in 1945 is a close second. The worst home opener may have been a 3-0 loss to New York in 1937.

 Name the right-winger who played for the New Jersey Devils and Pittsburgh Penguins before finding a home with the Red Wings in 1995.

 Doug Brown. He did well under coach Scotty Bowman, helping the team reach the Stanley Cup finals for the first time in nearly 30 years. Brown was utilized in a variety of situations as Detroit won consecutive titles in 1997 and 1998.

What rather famous football man was Brown's father-in-law?

 Wellington Mara, owner of the New York Giants.

 Name the Red Wings coaches between their 1955 Stanley Cup (Jimmy Skinner) and their 1997 Stanley Cup (Scotty Bowman).

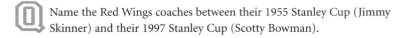 Sid Abel, Bill Gadsby, Ned Harkness, Doug Barkley, Johnny Wilson, Ted Garvin, Alex Delvecchio, Billy Dea, Larry Wilson, Bobby Kromm, Marcel Provonost, Ted Lindsay, Wayne Maxner, Nick Polano, Harry Neale, Brad Park, Jacques Demers, and Bryan Murray.

 How highly did the Red Wings prize Vladimir Konstantinov, a veteran of the Red Army team?

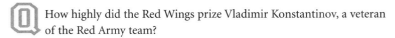 They had drafted him in 1989 and then used means that were either brilliant or unscrupulous to pry him away. In 1991, in an effort to expedite his discharge from the Russian army, the Red Wings allegedly bribed some Moscow doctors to say that Konstantinov had a rare form of cancer that could best be treated in the United States.

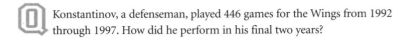

Konstantinov, a defenseman, played 446 games for the Wings from 1992 through 1997. How did he perform in his final two years?

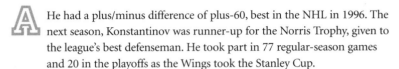

He had a plus/minus difference of plus-60, best in the NHL in 1996. The next season, Konstantinov was runner-up for the Norris Trophy, given to the league's best defenseman. He took part in 77 regular-season games and 20 in the playoffs as the Wings took the Stanley Cup.

It is unfortunate that Konstantinov is remembered less for what he did on the ice than for how his career ended. Recount that tragic matter.

A week after the Red Wings won the 1997 Cup, they had a party in a Detroit suburb. Konstantinov, teammate Viacheslav Fetisov, and team masseur Sergei Mnatsakanov were returning home in a limousine. The driver lost control of the vehicle and hit a tree. Fetisov and Mnatsakanov had relatively minor injuries, and the former was able to play the next season. But Konstantinov was comatose for a while and suffered brain damage. The 1998 Detroit team, which won the championship again, would wear a patch honoring their teammate.

Some observers thought he was the most versatile hockey player in the world in the 1990s. He excelled at center and on the wing, was a high scorer and fine defender and passer, a man who had mastered all aspects of the game. Name this Russian who did so much for the Wings for 13 seasons.

 Sergei Fedorov.

Fedorov was the second Soviet hockey player to defect (after Alexander Mogilny in 1989). What were the circumstances?

  Especially after his friend Mogilny's departure, he was under intense pressure to stay. But he took the opportunity when it arose. The Soviet team was in Seattle for the 1990 Goodwill Games when he went missing, to the consternation of his coach. Soon he had signed with the Red Wings, scoring 31 goals and making the 1991 all-rookie team.

When might it be said that Fedorov became a leader for the Red Wings?

  Perhaps in 1994 when Steve Yzerman was injured. He rallied his teammates, scored 56 goals, and won the Hart, Selke, and Pearson trophies. Coach Scotty Bowman asked for and got Viacheslav Fetisov and Igor Larionov the next year. Detroit had an all-Russian power play that featured Fedorov, Fetisov, Larionov, Konstantinov, and Vyacheslav Kozlov. The "Russian Five" had a lot to do with the Wings' back-to-back titles in 1997 and 1998. And, of course, Fedorov got another Stanley Cup in 2002.

Why were Fedorov's numbers (21 games, six goals) so small in 1998?

He missed most of the regular season in a contract dispute. But he was magnificent in the playoffs—22 games, 10 goals, 10 assists, and another championship. Fedorov later played with Anaheim and Columbus.

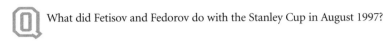

What did Fetisov and Fedorov do with the Stanley Cup in August 1997?

They and a couple of other Russian teammates took it for a jaunt in Red Square in Moscow.

This native of Barrie, Ontario, played for Detroit from 1987 to 1994 and was with the Carolina Hurricanes when they lost in the playoffs in 1999. Just hours after that final game, he died tragically. Who was he?

Steve Chiasson. He wrecked his pickup on the way home from a team party, killing himself instantly. According to teammates, Chiasson refused to call a taxi or accept a ride home, insisting on driving although his blood alcohol content of 0.27 was more than three times North Carolina's legal limit of 0.08. He left a wife and three kids.

How did the Wings do in the strike-shortened 1995 season?

They had the best record in the league at 33-11-4 and beat Dallas, San Jose, and Chicago en route to the Stanley Cup finals. But then they ran into a buzzsaw in the form of the New Jersey Devils and got swept.

This defenseman graduated from the University of Michigan in 1993 and cracked the Detroit lineup three years later. He was a mainstay with the Red Wings for five years and got a couple of Stanley Cup rings along the way. Name him.

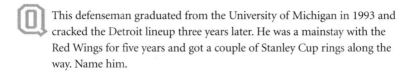 Aaron Ward. He was a member of the Carolina Hurricanes club that fell to Detroit in the 2002 Stanley Cup finals and later played for the New York Rangers.

 What team holds the NHL record for most wins (62) in a regular season?

The 1996 Detroit Red Wings.

 Name the gifted netminder from Peace River, Alberta, who led the NHL in 1996 with 39 wins.

Chris Osgood, one of the busiest and winningest goalies over the past decade, despite injuries and age. He spent eight years in Detroit and two each with the Islanders and Blues before being reacquired by the Wings in 2006.

 What did Osgood do in a 1996 game against the Hartford Whalers?

 He became the third goalie in NHL history to score a goal. It was an empty-net goal since the Whalers had sent all their players on the offensive in the final seconds.

 He had the good fortune to be surrounded by teammates like Yzerman, Fedorov, Fetisov, and Lidstrom when he joined the NHL in 1996. The next year, this solid defenseman was a part of the Wings' great playoff run to the title. Who is he?

Mathieu Dandenault, who also helped capture the Cup again in 1998 and 2002. He went to the Montreal Canadiens in 2006.

What left-winger, born in Guelph, Ontario, was traded to Detroit by the Edmonton Oilers and contributed five goals to the Red Wings' 1997 Stanley Cup victory?

Kirk Maltby. The next year, the hard-working forward scored a personal-best 14 goals as Detroit repeated as NHL champs. He has been a stellar player for the Wings for a decade now.

A favorite of fans at Joe Louis Arena for 11 seasons (1994–2004), this native of Burnaby, British Columbia, showed plenty of spunk as a left-winger. In 1997, his goal in the second period of Game 4 stood up as the clincher that brought Motown its first Stanley Cup in 42 years. He contributed 11 points when the Wings repeated as Cup winners the next season. Identify him.

Darren McCarty.

McCarty was an enforcer, known more for a ready use of his fists than his scoring ability. For what event is he best known?

They called it "Fight Night at the Joe." On March 26, 1997, the Red Wings and the Colorado Avalanche brawled. McCarty took out Avs right-winger Claude Lemieux, who had given Detroit forward Kris Draper a vicious hit in the playoffs the year before. McCarty went on to score the game-winning goal in overtime.

What former Red Wing now serves as Minister of Sport in Russia?

 Viacheslav "Slava" Fetisov, known also as the Russian Bobby Orr. One of the best defensemen of all time, the former captain of the Soviet Union national team helped break the barrier that had long prevented Soviet players from joining the NHL. On the international stage, Fetisov is among the most decorated players, winning two Olympic golds (1984 and 1988) and seven in the world championships (1978, 1981, 1982, 1983, 1986, 1989, and 1990). After 14 years with the CSKA Moscow club, Fetisov signed with the New Jersey Devils in 1989. He was with the Red Wings from 1995 to 1998, helping the team win two Stanley Cups. Following his retirement as a player, Fetisov won another as an assistant coach with the Devils in 2000.

 This fiery right-winger was born in Ville St-Pierre, Quebec, and spent most of the 1990s as a wearer of the Winged Wheel. His willingness to check and battle in the corners put him in coach Scotty Bowman's good graces, and he was an integral part of Detroit's 1997 and 1998 Stanley Cup titles. Who was he?

 Martin LaPointe, who later played with the Blackhawks and Bruins.

A native of Calgary, this goalie had been with the Flames for 12 years before coming to the Red Wings in 1995. He helped them reach the Stanley Cup finals against the New Jersey Devils that year and the semis in '96 against the Colorado Avalanche. Relegated to backing up Chris Osgood most of the season, he was back on the ice in the playoffs as Detroit won its first hockey championship in four decades. Who was he?

 Mike Vernon. Despite his sterling performance against Philadelphia, Vernon was soon dealt to the San Jose Sharks.

 Bob Rouse joined the Red Wings' blueline in 1995, after having played with the North Stars, the Capitals, and the Maple Leafs. How many goals did he score in four years with Detroit?

 Just six. Rouse was the prototypical stay-at-home defender, but he was quite adept at clearing creases.

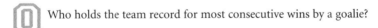

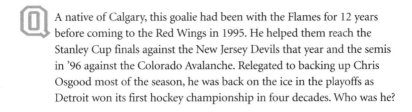 Who holds the team record for most consecutive wins by a goalie?

Chris Osgood, who won 13 straight in 1996.

133

This player with the flaming stick was chosen third overall by the Red Wings in the 1990 NHL draft, but some fans viewed him as an underachiever in his six seasons in the Motor City—notwithstanding the fact that he often had to play on the wing, which was not his natural position. Who was he?

 Keith Primeau. Not until he was traded to the Hartford Whalers (later the Carolina Hurricanes) did he become a front-line warrior, a strong skater with soft hands. He later played with the Flyers and represented Canada in the 1998 Winter Olympics. Primeau, who topped the 900-game, 600-point plateau, retired early in the 2006 season due to post-concussion syndrome.

 Name the right-winger who scored 1,200 points in his 19-year NHL career (mostly with the Minnesota North Stars), once pled guilty to indecent exposure, attacked a player (Luke Richardson of the Canadiens) with his stick and was convicted of assault, came close to winning a title with the Wings in 1995, and fought with the media after his retirement.

 Dino Ciccarelli. His combustible ways have not helped his chances of entering the Hockey Hall of Fame without paying admission.

 What two players share the record for most goals in a playoff season?

 Sergei Fedorov (19 games in 1996) and Steve Yzerman (22 games in 1998) both had 18.

Who was Detroit's most recent winner of the Vezina Trophy?

 Terry Sawchuk, back in 1955. However, Red Wings alumni Glenn Hall, Rogie Vachon, Ed Giacomin, and Dominik Hasek have won it for other teams.

 What native of Pitea, Sweden, was a utility man for Detroit's 1997 and 1998 Stanley Cup winners but had eight goals in 23 playoff games when the Wings won it again in '02?

 Tomas Holmstrom. A diligent worker at both ends of the ice, he had his best season in 2006, playing in 81 regular-season games and scoring 59 points.

 Detroit was up, 3-0, in the fourth game of the 1997 Stanley Cup finals against the Philadelphia Flyers. A Swedish-born player opened the scoring in what would be a 2-1 win, giving the Wings their first Stanley Cup in 42 years. Who was he?

Nicklas Lidstrom, a solid defender and rusher with powerful shots from the blueline. Winner of four Norris Trophies and one Conn Smythe, Lidstrom has been an NHL first-team All-Star six times. He has now played in more than 1,100 games for Detroit.

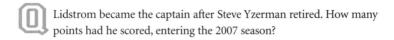

Lidstrom became the captain after Steve Yzerman retired. How many points had he scored, entering the 2007 season?

Lidstrom had 806 points. No doubt, he has had a lot to do with the Wings making the playoffs every season since his arrival in 1992.

This right-winger was an intimidating presence on the ice. He had become a regular with the Wings by 1986 and was a member of the New York Rangers when they won the 1994 Stanley Cup, their first in 54 years. Can you identify him?

Joe Kocur, who definitely played a robust, physical game. His career appeared to be winding down, as he was with a minor league team in San Antonio in 1997, until he got a call from the Red Wings' front office. In a limited role, Kocur helped the team win consecutive Stanley Cups in 1997 and 1998.

Four games into the 1996 season, the Wings acquired a 36-year-old center from the San Jose Sharks—a player with a glorious past but whom some considered to be over the hill. Who was he?

Igor Larionov, a center for the top team in the Soviet Union and winner of Olympic gold medals in 1984 and 1988. He was revered and welcomed in Detroit by countrymen Slava Fetisov, Sergei Fedorov, Vladimir Konstantinov, and Slava Kozlov. After the team won the 1997 Cup, captain Steve Yzerman first passed the prized trophy to Larionov.

How did Larionov's '98 debut go?

 He played in 69 games and had 39 assists, and the Red Wings repeated their feat by ousting the Washington Capitals in the Stanley Cup finals. The Detroit brass let him go to the Florida Panthers in 2001, but he was soon back with the Wings. In the twilight of his career, Larionov helped the team come flying out of the gate in 2002 and led the league from start to finish. In the Stanley Cup finals, the man his teammates called "the Professor" became the oldest player in NHL history to score a Stanley Cup finals goal when he notched one versus the Carolina Hurricanes. A small player at 5' 9" and 170 pounds, Larionov is considered one of the best passers the game has ever seen.

 Larry Murphy had one of the most productive careers of any blueliner in NHL history. Of what did it consist?

 This native of Scarborough, Ontario, was just 19 when he signed with the Los Angeles Kings, proceeding to set records in assists and point totals for a rookie defenseman. Murphy also had time in Washington, Minnesota, Pittsburgh (winning Stanley Cups in 1991 and 1992), and Toronto before signing with the Red Wings in 1997. Reinvigorated, Murphy was again part of back-to-back championships. He retired in 2001 after a sparkling 21-season career, which included eleven 60-point seasons. Murphy finished second all time in NHL games played (1,615), and third in assists (929) and points (1,216) by a defenseman. In 215 playoff games, he added 37 goals and 115 assists for 152 points.

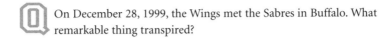

On December 28, 1999, the Wings met the Sabres in Buffalo. What remarkable thing transpired?

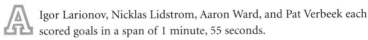

Igor Larionov, Nicklas Lidstrom, Aaron Ward, and Pat Verbeek each scored goals in a span of 1 minute, 55 seconds.

The Wings paid a steep price (defenseman Paul Coffey, forward Keith Primeau, and a first-round draft pick were sent to the Hartford Whalers) to get him early in the 1997 season. Who was this much-coveted hockey player?

Brendan Shanahan. A left-winger from the suburbs of Toronto, he was a star with the New Jersey Devils at the tender age of 22. He put in some very good years with the St. Louis Blues before being traded to Hartford and then Detroit; the latter trade was one he asked for. The Detroit Red Wings, who had been improving through wise trades and drafting, wanted Shanahan. Coach Scotty Bowman thought he could be the final element he needed to make the Wings a Cup winner after they lost in the 1995 finals to New Jersey and the 1996 semifinals to Colorado. Sure enough, Detroit captured the Stanley Cup in 1997 by sweeping the Philadelphia Flyers, then duplicated the feat in 1998 against the Washington Capitals. Shanahan maintained his strong play with the Wings, reaching the 500-goal and 1,000-point plateaus in 2002, and winning a third Cup by beating Carolina in five games.

What was "the Shanahan Summit"?

 Well-respected off the ice as well as on, Shanahan had become something of an elder statesman of hockey. He organized a two-day conference in Toronto during the NHL's lockout season of 2005; it brought together players, coaches, and others who cared about a game with a shaky long-term future. Ten recommendations were presented to the league and players' association.

 After a long career with the Devils, Whalers (where he was captain for four seasons), Rangers, and Stars, this right-winger came to Detroit, scoring 37 goals in 2000 and 2001. Who was he?

 Pat Verbeek. He played one more season in Dallas before giving up the game, having passed the 1,000-point mark.

 Verbeek, who was given the nickname "Little Ball of Hate" during his years in New York, later returned to the Red Wings organization in what capacity?

 As a broadcaster and a scout. Verbeek, by the way, is the only player in NHL history to score more than 500 goals and have 2,500 penalty minutes.

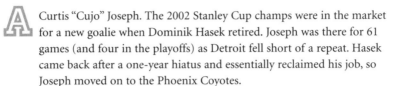

He spent one year at the University of Wisconsin and was a star while guarding the net of the St. Louis Blues, Edmonton Oilers, and Toronto Maple Leafs before signing with Detroit in 2003. Who was this goalie with a penchant for elevating his game in the NHL's second season?

Curtis "Cujo" Joseph. The 2002 Stanley Cup champs were in the market for a new goalie when Dominik Hasek retired. Joseph was there for 61 games (and four in the playoffs) as Detroit fell short of a repeat. Hasek came back after a one-year hiatus and essentially reclaimed his job, so Joseph moved on to the Phoenix Coyotes.

He was the 171st player selected in the 1984 NHL draft, the ninth chosen by the Los Angeles Kings. He soon proved the experts wrong as 1987 Calder Trophy winner and a highly prolific scorer for LA, Pittsburgh, the New York Islanders, and finally Detroit. Name this Montreal native.

Luc Robataille, who became a Red Wing for one reason—to win the Stanley Cup; that is exactly what happened in his first year (2002) in Detroit. He took part in 81 regular-season games and 23 playoff games, scoring a total of 59 points. Robataille's numbers were down in '03, however, and the Wings let him go back to Los Angeles. He retired in 2006 after 19 seasons of NHL competition as the highest-scoring left-winger in league history.

With their 2002 championship, the Wings had won the Stanley Cup 10 times. What two franchises do they trail?

The Montreal Canadiens (24) and the Toronto Maple Leafs (13).

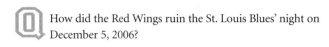 How did the Red Wings ruin the St. Louis Blues' night on December 5, 2006?

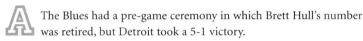 The Blues had a pre-game ceremony in which Brett Hull's number was retired, but Detroit took a 5-1 victory.

 Name the Red Wings who have scored more than 600 goals.

 Gordie Howe (801), Brett Hull (741), Marcel Dionne (731), Steve Yzerman (692), Luc Robataille (668), and Dino Ciccarelli (608).

Name the Red Wings who have recorded at least 800 career assists.

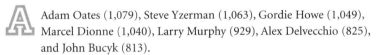 Adam Oates (1,079), Steve Yzerman (1,063), Gordie Howe (1,049), Marcel Dionne (1,040), Larry Murphy (929), Alex Delvecchio (825), and John Bucyk (813).

Name the Red Wings with at least 1,200 points in their careers.

Gordie Howe (1,850), Marcel Dionne (1,771), Steve Yzerman (1,755), Paul Coffey (1,531), Adam Oates (1,420), Luc Robataille (1,394), Brett Hull (1,391), John Bucyk (1,369), Alex Delvecchio (1,281), Brendan Shanahan (1,232), Norm Ullman (1,229), Larry Murphy (1,216), and Dino Ciccarelli (1,200).

Three Red Wings are in the NHL's top 20 of career goals per game. Who are they?

Brett Hull is fifth on the list at 0.58, Marcel Dionne is 12th at 0.54, and Dino Ciccarelli is 17th at 0.49.

 Name the Red Wings who are in the NHL's top 20 for career penalty minutes.

Dave "Tiger" Williams is far and away the leader in that dubious list; he sat out 3,966 minutes. Fifth is Bob Probert (3,300), 11th is Pat Verbeek (2,905), 12th is Chris Chelios (2,821), and 18th is Joe Kocur (2,519).

What Red Wings played in at least 1,300 games in their NHL careers?

Gordie Howe (1,767), Larry Murphy (1,615), Alex Delvecchio (1,549), John Bucyk (1,540), Steve Yzerman (1,514), Chris Chelios (1,476), Luc Robataille (1,431), Pat Verbeek (1,424), Norm Ullman (1,410), Dean Prentice (1,378), Brendan Shanahan (1,350), Marcel Dionne (1,348), Adam Oates (1,337), and Red Kelly (1,316).

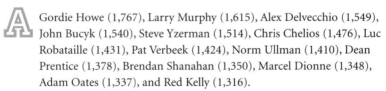

What Detroit goalies have had at least 40 career shutouts?

Terry Sawchuk (103), Glenn Hall (84), Alex Connell (81), Tiny Thompson (81), Harry Lumley (71), Dominik Hasek (68), John Ross Roach (58), Ed Giacomin (54), Rogie Vachon (51), Curtis Joseph (47), and Chris Osgood (43).

Name the Red Wings goalies who have at least 300 career wins.

 Terry Sawchuk (447), Curtis Joseph (428), Glenn Hall (407), Mike Vernon (385), Rogie Vachon (355), Harry Lumley (330), Chris Osgood (325), and Dominik Hasek (324).

 According to *Forbes Magazine,* how much money did the Red Wings lose in 2004, prior to the lockout season?

 $16 million.

 Did the Red Wings have a player on the NHL All-Star team in 2006?

 Yes—Nicklas Lidstrom, who also won the Norris Trophy as the best defenseman in the league.

 And what Detroit player won the 2006 Lady Byng Trophy for sportsmanship?

 Pavel Datsyuk. Other Byng Trophy winners include Marty Berry (1936), Bill Quackenbush (1949), Red Kelly (1951, 1953, and 1954), Dutch Reibel (1956), Alex Delvecchio (1959, 1966, and 1969), and Marcel Dionne (1975).

 What Red Wing was on the 2006 all-rookie team?

None of them. The team consisted of Henrik Lundquist of the Rangers, Brad Boyes of the Bruins, Sidney Crosby of the Penguins, Alexander Ovechkin of the Capitals, Andrej Meszaros of the Senators, and Dion Phaneuf of the Flames.

How did goaltender Manny Legace do in the '06 season?

He played 2,905 minutes in 51 games, gave up 106 goals (an average of 2.19 a game—third best in the league), and had 7 shutouts, for a record of 37-8-3.

Two employees of a Detroit sports bar were murdered during the 2007 season. What Red Wings player owned the establishment?

Defenseman Chris Chelios, owner of Cheli's Chili Bar.

Why was the Detroit–Anaheim game on January 2, 2007 (a 2-1 Wings victory) delayed for more than an hour?

It was so "the Captain," Steve Yzerman, could have his No. 19 jersey retired before an adoring crowd at Joe Louis Arena. A team captain for an NHL-record 20 seasons, Yzerman was widely regarded as a great leader and a classy competitor.

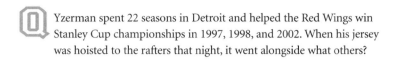 Yzerman spent 22 seasons in Detroit and helped the Red Wings win Stanley Cup championships in 1997, 1998, and 2002. When his jersey was hoisted to the rafters that night, it went alongside what others?

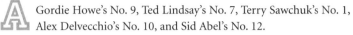 Gordie Howe's No. 9, Ted Lindsay's No. 7, Terry Sawchuk's No. 1, Alex Delvecchio's No. 10, and Sid Abel's No. 12.

 Entering the 2007 season, five Red Wings have scored more than 100 points in the NHL playoffs. Who are they?

Steve Yzerman (185), Sergei Fedorov (163), Gordie Howe (158), Nicklas Lidstrom (118), and Alex Delvecchio (104).

Lidstrom is obviously the leader of present-day playoff scoring leaders for Detroit. Who trails him?

 Tomas Holstrom (54), Kris Draper (38), Kirk Maltby (27), and Chris Chelios (21).

Seven Detroit goaltenders have won more than 10 games in the playoffs. Who are they?

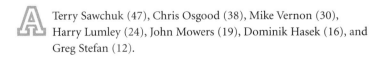 Terry Sawchuk (47), Chris Osgood (38), Mike Vernon (30), Harry Lumley (24), John Mowers (19), Dominik Hasek (16), and Greg Stefan (12).

What happened in franchise history on January 4, 2007?

 The Red Wings, who had been ahead, 3-0, gave up six power-play goals (a team record) in a 9-4 loss to the San Jose Sharks. *Detroit News* writer Ted Kulfan called it "an utter embarrassment," and few of the players disagreed.

 Entering the 2007 season, what team had the Wings faced most often through the years?

 The Chicago Blackhawks (681 games), followed by the Toronto Maple Leafs (638), the Boston Bruins (572), the New York Rangers (570), and the Montreal Canadiens (562). They, along with the Red Wings, constitute the Original Six of the National Hockey League.

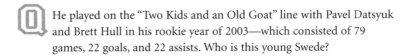

 He played on the "Two Kids and an Old Goat" line with Pavel Datsyuk and Brett Hull in his rookie year of 2003—which consisted of 79 games, 22 goals, and 22 assists. Who is this young Swede?

Henrik Zetterberg. A finalist for the Calder Trophy in '03, he has done nothing but shine for Detroit and his home country ever since. Zetterberg, an alternate captain (Nick Lidstrom wears the "C"), scored the 100th goal of his pro career on February 7, 2007, in a 4-2 defeat of Phoenix. He and his Swedish compatriots won a gold medal in the 2006 Winter Olympics and then again in the 2006 World Championship in Riga.

Are the Red Wings going to stay at Joe Louis Arena?

 Ever since the summer of 2006, there have been persistent rumors in Detroit that the Red Wings might leave "the Joe" for a new arena. Although Mike Ilitch and his family (his wife and daughters are quite involved in the operation of the team, too) have not confirmed any such plans, they appointed Randy Lippe as the new head of arena development. His duties involve researching a renovation of Joe Louis Arena, as well as the construction of a brand-new rink—whether in downtown Detroit or in the suburbs. Some fans, perhaps many, insist the Joe needs to go, calling it old, outdated, and inconvenient.

 How many times have the Red Wings made it into the NHL playoffs?

 As of the 2007 season, 16 straight times—the longest active streak in any pro sport.

 Who did the Wings beat to advance to the 2007 Western Conference finals?

 They closed out the San Jose Sharks in six games. In the series clincher at the Shark Tank, goalie Dominik Hasek stopped all 28 shots that came his way, and Mikael Samuelsson had a pair of first-period goals.

Some hockey fans considered Detroit one of the biggest playoff under-achievers in the previous three years, winning at least 48 games each time only to falter in the postseason. So how did Mike Babcock's team fare in the next round against Anaheim?

The Ducks won it in six games. In the last one, Anaheim built a 3-0 lead but the Wings stormed back in the final period with three goals of their own. Samuel Pahlsson's goal proved to be the difference for Anaheim. Randy Carlyle's club would go on to beat the Ottawa Senators to win the '07 Stanley Cup.

 Within a month after being bounced from the 2007 playoffs, the Red Wings got some good news about two aging but valuable players. Who were they?

The players in question were 45-year-old defenseman Chris Chelios and 42-year-old goalie Dominik Hasek. Both agreed to come back and try their best to bring another title to Hockeytown.

 The Ducks were the first West Coast team to win the cup in a very long time. Who preceded them?

The 1925 Victoria Cougars who, as we know, would soon move to Detroit and become the Red Wings.